# DEALING WITH GENERATION WASTERS

(Divine Insight Into The Operations Of Spirits Of Destruction)

## BY

## TAIWO OLUSEGUN AYENI

authorHOUSE™

*1663 LIBERTY DRIVE, SUITE 200*
*BLOOMINGTON, INDIANA 47403*
*(800) 839-8640*
*WWW.AUTHORHOUSE.COM*

© 2005 TAIWO OLUSEGUN AYENI. All Rights Reserved.

No part of this book may be reproduced, stored in a retrieval system, or transmitted by any means without the written permission of the author.

First published by AuthorHouse 01/25/05

ISBN: 1-4208-1794-9 (sc)

Printed in the United States of America
Bloomington, Indiana

This book is printed on acid-free paper.

All scriptures in this book are from King James Version
Of the Bible, unless otherwise indicated.
Rehoboth Ministries Publications
2822 S. State Highway 360 APT 925
Grand Prairie, Texas 75052, USA
(972) 602-1837
(972) 742-7365

Or

The Household of Faith Parish
The Redeemed Christian Church of God
5001 New York Avenue,
Arlington Texas, 76018, USA
Tel.:1-817-461-8857
Fax: 817-676-9067
E-mail: taayeni@yahoo.com

# Dedication

I dedicate this book to the Almighty God who prepared for me a dwelling place.

# Acknowledgements

I wish to thank God that after a series of prolonged interruption this book is eventually out. The demands of ministry coupled with the need to meet up with certain challenges of life hindered the progress of work.

The unavailability of a laptop computer to use on my numerous ministry trips and relocation to the United States slowed down the pace of work. I thank God for Pastor & Pastor (Mrs.) Ebenezer Ropo Tusin of Household of Faith, Arlington, Texas who did not only bless me with a notebook computer but hosted my family and I for several months on our 'first missionary journey'. This gift gave the work a major boost and confirmed to me that God does not expect excuses any more but performance. To them I say 'Thank you.'

The Lord gave me 'on the job transfer' to this nation and the Lord used many wonderful people whose names are not mentioned here to make my stay comfortable. I pray that as you encouraged me to find my footing in this country the Lord himself will encourage you all.

However, I wish to specifically thank my amiable wife Dr. (Mrs.) Abidemi Olubisi Ayeni, Pastor & Pastor (Mrs.) Olusegun Osunsan, Dr & Mrs. Wole Odumade, Ms Gbemi Joseph for their various contributions. God bless and keep you till the coming of our king, the Lord Jesus Christ. Amen.

# TABLE OF CONTENTS

Dedication .................................................................... v
Acknowledgements ................................................... vii
Preface ........................................................................ xi
FOREWORD ............................................................. xv

Chapter One
GENERATION WASTER. ........................................ 1

Chapter Two
THE ROOT OF AFFLICTIONS ............................. 21

Chapter Three
THE OPERATIONS OF GENERATION WASTERS? ........ 43

Chapter Four
MANIFESTATIONS OF GENERATION WASTERS ......... 61

Chapter Five
DEALING WITH GENERATION WASTERS ..................... 75

Chapter Six
THE GENERATION OF WICKEDNESS? ........................ 101

Chapter Seven
DEALING WITH THE TROUBLES OF LIFE .................. 117

Chapter Eight
TAKE DOMINION ................................................. 139

Chapter Nine
POSSESSING YOUR POSSESSIONS ............................ 163

Chapter Ten
UPON MOUNT ZION ............................................ 177

Appendix .................................................................. 193

# Preface

I have often wondered why the imbalances we witness in life exist at all, not to mention why it persists. Somehow, some families are faced with certain inexplicable problems that waste their clan even before their time. It is like a spiritual barrier that limits men from making it in life. The picture of happenings within the church of God if graphically drawn is an ominous one. It is so hopeless that the accounts are indeed frightening.

Many innocent and kind-hearted people suffer due to faults that are not theirs. When one looks at the whole picture of the kinds of suffering men go through in life one wonders why. One thing that is however clear is that demonic entities do not operate in men's lives without legal reasons. As a result many families are bound and heavily afflicted without any hope of deliverance by 'lawful captivity'. If they had had an idea of the battle against their lives, they should have at least sought for help from those who could help them draw strategic spiritual battle plans

Ignorance has continued to be a major weapon the enemy wields against his victims. The enemy is having a field day by taking advantage of peoples' weaknesses and attacking them from the position of knowledge. This has left many souls thoroughly abused, tormented, used, harassed, and embarrassed. This is because they have been made to believe, in their weakness and ignorance that there is no hope of deliverance.

The morbid encounters they experienced left lasting impression in the hearts that there is no hope in sight and they passionately believe it.

This lie of Satan has made them resign to fate and believe nothing could be done about it. Some see it as family problems, which they have prepared themselves and their children to accept with equanimity. You hear them proudly saying that 'It runs in the family'. The fact that cancer, heart disease, diabetes, asthma etc had over the years easily and successfully destroyed several generations of family members, while others seeing no way out of it are prepared for the same affliction.

This is not supposed to be so because there is a way out in Christ Jesus. The name of the Lord is a strong tower the righteous runs into it and they are safe. With consistent targeted spiritual warfare prayers the situation should long have been overcome.

***'He delivereth the poor in his affliction, and openeth their ears in oppression. Even so would he have moved thee out of the strait into a broad place, where there is no straitness; and that which should be set on thy table should be full of fatness.'*** (Job 36:15-16).

This work is a follow up to my two books **'*Fighting Your Way to Victory*** – *principles of victory over stubborn problems'* which deals with the revival of one's prayer life, and **'*Smashing the Gates of the Enemy*** – *through Strategic Prayers'* which encourages the believer to engage in strategic spiritual warfare in order to unseat the powers of darkness limiting them from entering into their inheritance. The book is titled ***'Dealing with Generation Wasters'.***

It reveals the operations of generation wasters in men's lives and tries to explain why many people have experienced untold hardships and sufferings that are beyond human comprehension. The kinds of sufferings some go through makes one to believe they are better of dead than alive. It is such that makes a graduate, with obvious opportunities in life to end up as a menial worker. This regular sequence of events is passed down from generation to generation with varied degrees of wickedness and sufferings. They have experienced a history of failure at the point of success and every attempt to go higher is thwarted by invisible barriers unknown to them.

The generation wasters with the assistance of spiritual gates have defined the limits of people's success and how far they can go in life. In order for them to break this barrier, there must be divine intervention. The first step towards victory is to comprehend what the problem is, acknowledge it, and seek for help. Some have failed to accept the situation on ground, but continue to pretend, even after the facts have been made clear to them through personal and realistic assessment of their lives.

While, it is obvious to all that they are bound, yet they carry on as if nothing is happening. This is the reason for the number of casualties being recorded in our various churches, as many die before their time because they fail to seek for help. There is a need to wage spiritual war through unrelenting prayers. This requires a cry between the porch and the altar till we see change. We should do this with diligence and militant stride in order to give the enemy no breathing space. Deliverance is available to those who are willing to pay the price.

My prayer is that this book should help you open the door that would lead you into entering other doors to truth as you search. This book is not the truth, neither is it the total answer to man's spiritual problems. It is only a guide that will challenge you to take a second look at your problems and rise up to tackle it. You can make it rise up and fight. God bless you.

Taiye Ayeni

# FOREWORD

The word of God says in *Ps. 11:3* that *"If the foundations be destroyed, what can the righteous do?."* Many people, including numerous Christians are suffering from what I call "Abnormal Struggle Syndrome (ASS)" today because their foundations have been tampered with by the troubles and trials addressed in this book.

The activities of 'Generation Wasters' are real. As a Pastor, I have been counselling people concerning spiritual matters for some years now, and I can tell you that I have seen many whose destinies were being wasted by the wickedness of Generation wasters. The good news is that I have also seen many delivered from the activities of these destiny destroyers through the ministry of our Lord Jesus Christ.

Are you going through peculiar problems (i.e. beyond human understanding)? Are you worried about a particular problem that seems to run through generations before you in your father or mother's side of family or both, such as barrenness, early death or particular sicknesses? Are you concerned that you labour so much only to reap little or nothing? Are you tired of a life that is stagnated and curiously limited? Do you always miss good things just when you are at the edge of breakthrough? Have you noticed any abnormal character trait or negative habit that runs through your family? Do you just feel convinced that you need a clear insight into real issues of life? If you or any one known to you answers yes to any of these questions, then I must tell you that this is a must read book for you.

The author has written what I would call a Compendium of Spiritual Warfare. This book takes you from the reality of the problem and leads you straight to the strategies for victory. This book will help the reader overcome the problem of ignorance in vital areas of life. Your understanding of the issues presented in this book will make you outstanding and fulfilled in the purpose of the Creator and Giver of Life.

I have been personally blessed reading the manuscripts and I have no doubt that every reader will have testimonies to share to the glory of God. I commend Pastor Ayeni's thoroughness, toughness and tenacity in making this great piece available to our world.

*Leke Sanusi*

*Pastor, The Redeemed Christian Church of God (RCCG) Victory House, London*

# Chapter One
# GENERATION WASTER.

*'....I created the waster to destroy.' - Is. 54:16*

## *What are Generation Wasters?*

The generation wasters are satanic entities that consistently operate with unbroken coalition with spiritual gates. Before we deliberate on Generation Wasters, it is important to first examine what spiritual gates are.

Spiritual gates or gatekeepers are men who have unusual supernatural powers to hinder men from entering into their inheritance in life. The Bible gives us insight into the fact that men can actually shut out others from their inheritance because of the spiritual powers they have acquired over time. This entity of darkness exercises authority over his victims either positively (for good) or negatively (for evil), because of the supernatural power he possesses. If he pleases he allows certain category of people to enter into their inheritances, while he hinders others from enjoying this privilege.

Because he holds the territorial power of attorney to take decisions that are binding upon the people, most of the time he afflicts and oppresses them. He denies men the good things of life by erecting invisible barriers in their path to hinder them just like territorial spirits do. In a nutshell spiritual gates cause sorrow, tears and bloodshed to their hapless victims all over the world.

## *The influence of Territorial Spirits*

The generation wasters in collaboration with spiritual gates are more or less territorial in nature. These spirits specialize in wasting the lives and properties of people in their geographical domain. The initial trap is the allegiance to the community gods, traditional festivals, and ceremonies routinely done in such communities. Some communities have certain traditional rites they offer to appease the gods of the land and some families are custodians and worshippers of these gods.

Some rites are mandatorily done at birth, naming, marriage, birthday, and town day ceremonies. Commonly practiced in the recent past were tribal marks or tattoos that make the people known by sight from people of other communities. These marks are

## DEALING WITH GENERATION WASTERS

known to differ from community to community and are specified by territorial powers as tokens of covenants between them and the people. Specifically, these marks are tokens of blood covenants with the territorial powers ruling over the community.

Through these activities they afflict generations of people with the same problems within a community and also down the family line. This becomes possible because every one involved in such traditional activities is automatically under the curse of God and they suffer what is identified as generational or inherited curses and afflictions. The book of Psalm Chapter 97 verse 7 says ***'Confounded be all they that put their trust in idols..'***

There are communities where the people are noted for promiscuity, while others are largely untrustworthy. In the first, it is a known fad that a woman never dies married to one man. The usual scenario is that a woman may have four children with each having different fathers and is still in the business of having an alarming high turnover of lover boys.

A particular life example reveals a home where a grand mother (who was a single mother) lived with her daughter (also a single mother) and has a grand daughter whose favorite pastime was offering herself as 'a universal donor' to anything in pants. This grand child, just barely out of the cradle, was well known to have broken every sense of restraints in the book and matched every adjective that her preys used to qualify her. Very soon she ended the same way those before her did, a single mother.

In case of those who are untrustworthy, when they tell you something you better put a rain check on it, or you may pay dearly for it because you can never find them to be reliable. The degree of affliction per family or person within the community may differ, but they are all generally the same. As per individual curses the way and manner in which great grand father was afflicted, was the same way grandfather suffered and now in the fourth generation the great grand child now a father is under the same affliction.

The spirits afflicting them file away documents of satanic contracts or transactions and use them effectively, when the need arises, to deal legally with their victims. These documents are reference points to the activities of the past, the promises made and responsibilities tied to it. The covenant or contracts of the forefathers have put several generations, born and unborn into perpetual bondage. Where there is default to these contracts or agreements the satanic entities move viciously against their recalcitrant but helpless victims in order to enforce compliance.

It is however important to mention that the basic legal power backing these powers are the altars raised by the fathers knowingly or unknowingly while entering into satanic contracts or covenants with them. Several things can be used to raise altars and enter into covenants. These same items used to raise altars can conversely become altars of affliction against the person that raised the altar in the first place. These include blood, hair, clothing, fingernails, body parts, photographs, effigy, drinks, food, etc. These essentially are tokens of covenants presented to afflict whosoever is the owner or from whose body they were taken from.

The demons that supervise the execution of these covenants or contracts are called covenant enforcers. They work with the generation wasters to mete out necessary punishments to violators of the covenants. We have seen them in operation in various parts of the Bible, they are always ruthless and without mercy. In short, their specific assignment is to steal, kill, and destroy.

However, the church of Christ must be built, and the gates of hell shall not prevail against it. Why do the demons mentioned above defy spiritual solutions that have worked for others with impunity? What have given these spirits so much audacity that they refuse to bow even under intense prayers and put forward heavy resistance on such occasions? Where do their strength lie and how is this renewed? These are some of the issues to be examined in this chapter. (Please refer to **Smashing the Gates of the enemy** – *through strategic prayers*, by the same author for detailed information on Spiritual Gates.)

## *Understanding Generation Wasters*

### *i) The kings and people of Israel and Judah*
The study of the kings and people of Israel and Judah will enable us to understand better the operation of Generation Wasters. As mentioned earlier on, this set of demons work in a family lineage with the sole aim

of totally destroying it. We saw them in operations in the lineages of Jeroboam the son of Nebat, Baasha the son of Ahijah, and Ahab the son of Omri to mention just a few.

These spirits seduced the kings and people to commit sin in order to make them prone to spirits of destruction and thereby waste their generations. The kings and their people in almost all the cases fell for these traps, and God in several instances reacted in response to their wickedness by bringing justified judgment on them. However, when God's judgment is logically analyzed, one will discover that it does not affect only the man that sinned alone, but also his posterity. For example, in dealing with the sins of Ahab we read this account:

> ***'Behold, I will bring evil upon thee, and will take away thy posterity...'*** (I Kings 21:21-22).

It is painful to know that this happened to innocent souls who were not partakers in the sins of these wicked men. However, this was God's way of cleansing the generation and wiping out evil from the land. It holds true that the fruit that evil bears is also likely to be evil. Hence God cuts them down before they become problems to the nation.

It is pertinent to mention here that God is not always quick to punish, but full of mercy and gracious. However, when one sits down to think about the kind of things these men did and the legitimacy they gave evil, it is then one can appreciate the fact that God really endured them for too long. Their capacities to imagine wickedness in their hearts and execute them without mercy convincingly prove that they were under the control of evil spirits.

The fact that they were involved with such unthinkable degree of wickedness revealed the level at which the spirit of destruction had possessed them. Words will not be enough to describe the depth to which these men had sank in passionate embrace of wickedness. No wonder the pattern and regularity of wickedness were alarmingly consistent to the point in which the common refrain during this period was:

*'And he did evil in the sight of the Lord, and walked in the way of his father, and in his sin wherewith he made Israel to sin'* - (I Kings 15:26)

The plan of the devil to ruin every king that sat upon the throne and made him to have no credibility had its strong foundation laid in the time of Jeroboam. It was nurtured, well refined through some of the kings who reigned after Jeroboam, but was despicably articulated and institutionalized by Ahab. The Bible simply handed over the trophy of grandiose wickedness and evil to Ahab unopposed, as he had no competitor in sight:

*'But there was none like unto Ahab, which did sell himself to work wickedness in the sight of the Lord, whom Jezebel his wife stirred up.'* (I Kings 21:25)

## ii) *The Wasting of The Royal Seeds*

The level of wickedness during the period under focus was mind-boggling. It was as if the kings and the people were competing for trophies in the demonstration of wickedness. There were several coups, assassinations, mass murder, arson and so on and so forth. It was a period of total anarchy.

During this period, several kings did not have the opportunity to settle down to rule because of treachery and unexpected killings of the king's tribe. When one briefly takes a quick run through II Kings Chapters 9 to 11, one will be surprised at the number of lives wasted as a result of the satanic domination of this period. Several innocent souls were snuffed out before their times. The Kings' tribe and the people suffered untold hardship during this time. Even though the list is endless find below selected portions of deaths and destructions of the kings family.

1. Jehoram the son of Ahab (II Kings 9:24-25)

2. Jezebel (II Kings 9:30-37)

3. Seventy (70) sons of the king ( II Kings 10:7-8)

4. Ahab's great men, kinfolks, priests, and all that remained in his house in Jezreel until none was left. ( II Kings 10:11; ref I King 21:19-21)

5. Forty two brethren of Ahaziah (II Kings 10:13-14)

6. He slew all that remained of Ahab in Samaria, till he had destroyed him (II Kings 10:17)

7. All the worshippers of Baal (II Kings 10:18-28)

8. All the seed royal destroyed by Athaliah because of Ahaziah's death (II Kings 11:1)

9. Athaliah herself was killed (II Kings 11:13-16, 20).

### *iii) Africa's Ruling Princes*

The unfailing agenda of Generation Wasters all of the time is to kill, steal, and destroy. We can see them at work in living colors, achieving the three specified unfailing agenda through the kings as we study I kings 16:8-28. The same method of the seduction of kings in order to fall out of favor with God and thereby be prone to destruction is also found in several nations especially Africa, where through coups and political rivalry many generations have been and are still been wasted.

However, because *'Wisdom is too high for a fool: he openeth not his mouth in the gate'* (Prov 24:7), many who are supposed to know the truth downplay the happenings around them. It is pertinent at this point however, to introduce a summarized quotation from TELL Magazine (one of the leading magazines published in Nigeria) of April 8th 1996 in a commentary on sit tight leaders:

**'Once at the totem pole of power, African ruling elites seem to contract the Methuselah enzyme for longevity'**

Several African leaders analyzed by this magazine are listed below:

i) Henry Boigny (Ivory Coast) was replaced by Konan Bedied through the help of DEATH.

ii) Kamuzu Banda (Malawi) at the age of 90, battling with brain surgery refused to leave until he was defeated and replaced by Bakili Muluzi.

iii) Gnassingbe Eyadema (Togo) still held on to power as at April 1996 after more than 20 years in office.

iv) Kenneth Kaunda (Zambia) reigned for 27 years until Chiluba Frederick sent him packing through the polls.

v) Kenya's Daniel Arap Moi in order to remain perpetually in power prevented his strong opponent Richard Leakey from being registered.

vi) Robert Mugabe (Zimbabwe) used to be the darling president of the country is now doing all sorts to remain in power.

vii) Yakubu Gowon (Nigeria) ruled for many years until he was shamefully removed.

viii) Ibrahim Badamasi Babangida wept like a baby when he had to leave in August 1993. He held on to power for eight years.

These men have all played the fools. They did everything including fetish powers to remain in government. Yet God is angry every day for innocent blood being shed in nations. Even the blood is crying for vengeance. Hence we see a continuous cycle of deaths and destructions in most nations where such evils thrive. God's anger has procured for them and their posterity curses that would wipe out their generations in order to uproot evil from the land. A confirmation of this is recorded in Hosea 9:12-14:

*'Though they bring up their children, yet will I bereave them, that there shall not be a man left: yea, woe also to them when I depart from them!*

They are

*'..planted in pleasant place: but... shall bring forth his children to the murderer. Give them, O Lord: what wilt thou give? Give them a miscarrying womb and dry breasts.'*

## Get To The Roots

It has been observed that, most of the time when dealing with this spirit the physical is usually concentrated upon, while the spiritual root is untouched and left intact. For example, God raised Jehu to finish the house of Ahab and the remnants. There is no doubt that he did a good job of it – he killed the men, but never touched the spirit controlling them. This means that the root cause of evil was still very intact.

Why is this so? It is simply because he had no spiritual capacity to handle this problem. As a result the same set of evil spirits caught up with him and messed up his testimony. The very cancer he fought to destroy came over him and spread into every organ of his life until he was rejected by God. (II Kings 10:28-29):

*'Thus Jehu destroyed Baal out of Israel. Howbeit from the sins of Jeroboam the son of Nebat, who made Israel to sin, Jehu departed not from after them, to wit, the golden calves that were in Bethel and that were in Dan.'*

Jehu fell under the spiritual attack of forces of destruction that he once passionately fought against, so much that the powers seduced him and won him over to do evil. He became so ensnared that the zeal he had for God literarily frizzled away. He literally sank into the abyss of temporary insanity, for how else should one describe the actions of this man who specifically began to have attractions for the golden calves that were both in Bethel and Dan to worship them. His heart completely shifted to the side of evil that the bible has this to say about him in II Kings 10:31:

*But Jehu took no heed to walk in the law of the Lord God of Israel with all his heart: for he*

***departed not from the sins of Jeroboam, which made Israel to sin.***

Why was this so? This is because you do not handle cases like this without strong prayer backing. The enemies will usually fight back and when they do one will be twice worse than the object of sin he was pitched against.

## *Identifying Wasters*

In order for us to clearly identify these demons, we have classified them into three operational parts. These are familiar, ancestral, or territorial generation wasters.

**i) Familiar**
Where familiar spirits are at work the affliction is peculiar to a member of the family. This is distinctively obvious, as other members of the family do not suffer this fate. The case is familiar to the person involved. Hence so many members of the person's family will be doing very well, but the victim will be like an enigma as he or she suffers untold hardship.

One key point to note is the contradiction in the whole situation. This is the fact that even though the victim works harder than the members of his family that are doing well he remains alarmingly poor. This usually opens the eyes of onlookers to know that some powers are at work against the victim.

There is the pitiable story of one of the wives in a polygamous family in Africa who suffered untold hardship in her husband's home. The enemy wiped her out completely to the point in which she could not sustain any viable business except selling pap. All other high profit yielding projects she handled ended up in disaster as her daily sales kept disappearing from where she kept them. The experience brought a reproach upon her and her children as they live in penury in the midst of a vast ocean of material prosperity.

A biblical example of familiar waster is the story of Rachel. It is very clear that her lineage enjoyed longevity and many of them died in their good old age. That was not to be for Rachel. What happened? Her husband Jacob foolishly spoke a word that backfired on his beloved wife.

Unknown to him Rachel had stolen her father's gods and the man pursued them (Jacob, Rachel and the entire family) in order to recover them. In response to Laban's accusation, Jacob in a state of self-righteousness foolishly said:

*"With whomsoever thou findest thy gods, let him not live..."* (Gen. 31:32).

Jacob made this statement with the assurance that none of his family members had the gods yet verse 32 of Genesis 31 reads

*'..For Jacob knew not that Rachel had stolen them.'*

## *DEALING WITH GENERATION WASTERS*

What a pity! His statement however proved very costly because he opened up the door for Rachel's untimely death. The curse became effective because there was a strong reason for it – the gods stolen by Rachel. It robbed one of the seed's of Abraham her inherited longevity.

In a nutshell, the enemy capitalized on the edge broken by stealing her father's gods and the serpent bit her. Contrary to God's promise to the Jewish women at delivery we read that *". ...Rachel travailed, and she had hard labour."* (Gen. 35:16).

Her husband, who ought to have known better in careless overconfidence sold out the destiny of his wife through swear words. Consequently, we read that:

*"...Rachel died, and was buried in the way to Ephrath which is Bethlehem."* (Gen. 35:19).

This woman died at the edge of success. She experienced death very close to her destination and never made it to the land of promise as she was wasted in the way.

Another example is Lot's wife, who probably had a lot of worldly acquisitions left behind in Sodom; hence her heart was where her treasures were. We saw in Genesis 19, how her greed or covetousness made her to look back despite God's warning. The book of Luke 17:32 in warning us not to fall into the same trap tells us in simple but three profound words

*"Remember Lot's wife"*

What is there to remember about her? She became a prey in the hands of generation wasters, in her carelessness to sustain worldly gains at the expense of godly living. In spite of all she had heard about the faithfulness of the God of the Hebrews, this should not matter. She just must help herself, as some erroneously believe that 'Heavens help those who help themselves'. What a costly lie and hence the enemy cut short her promising life because of the judgment of the wicked. The Bible says that:

*'..their foot shall slide in due time: for the day of their calamity is at hand, and the things that shall come upon them make haste'* (Deut. 32:35)

Why is this so? It is because God *'...didst set them in slippery places:'* (Ps. 73:18).

### ii) Ancestral

The manifestation of ancestral spirits affect majority of the family members say at least three out of five persons. This becomes glaring as they all begin to exhibit common unbelievable traits irrespective of their age. For example, when Abraham got to Egypt, he lied; when Isaac got to Gerar, he lied and Jacob lied with impunity to survive in life.

Furthermore, it is observed that there are four generations of barrenness identified in Abraham's family line. Please find these itemized below:

## *DEALING WITH GENERATION WASTERS*

i) Sarah - *'But Sarai was <u>barren</u>; she hath no child'* (Gen. 11:30).

ii) Rebekah – *'And Isaac entreated the Lord for his wife, because she was <u>barren</u>: and the Lord was entreated of him, and Rebekah his wife conceived.'* (Gen. 25:21).

iii) Leah – *'And when the Lord saw that Leah was hated, he <u>opened</u> her womb…'* (Gen. 29:31).

iv) Rachel – *'And God remembered Rachel, and he <u>opened</u> her womb.'* (Gen. 30:22).

Notice the common phrase used for both Leah and Rachel - '…*he <u>opened</u> her womb.*' If their wombs were not shut, there would have been no need to open them. The four women down the ancestral line suffered in the hand of the devil. This is family line or ancestral affliction.

There was the story of a man who built four chalets for his married daughters. Unknown to him these became snares for the ladies, to the point in which any little quarrel would elicit packing there things to return home. One by one the four of them, terminated their marriages and ended the business in their individual chalets as divorcees. The ancestral spirits used the chalets as the attractions that ruined the marriage.

### iii) Territorial

Territorial spirit manifestations affect a substantial number of the families in the community where they operate. As a result they will all begin to exhibit common traits of afflictions. The presence of these unseen forces of darkness and their visible consorts put the people in bondage through various subtle means such as village ceremonies and the revival of age long but dead traditional rites.

The observance of these rites binds the people to pledges that cost them their freedom. In such communities where this is the case the atmosphere is always tense and matters that ordinarily should be settled communally usually degenerate into inexplicable violence. A good example is the communal clashes you see happening in some parts of Africa. When one sits down to investigate the root cause of these clashes, one realizes with shock that they are mostly not issues that should draw blood. The truth is that they are spiritually inspired, and they have deeper spiritual depths that both the government and the people can neither comprehend nor handle.

In most cases, it was the result of covenant rites or satanic sacrifices made by their forefathers that continue to cause harvest of deaths and destructions for the people. They have not experienced fresh season of respite because their victims' blood is crying for vengeance. For example, there was a community where nothing good ever entered. An evangelist born and bred in this community tried all he could to influence spiritual and physical changes all to no avail. While he pondered on why his crusades in other communities were highly successful and those he did in his own community were studies in organized failures, the Lord opened his eyes to a source of solution.

He was inspired to meet one of the oldest men in the community. The man revealed to him how two white men bringing the gospel into the community were arrested, detained, humiliated, and gruesomely killed. Before they buried them in a shallow grave they removed their hearts, went to the center of the town, buried their hearts there and planted a tree on top of them for a sign. While they were burying the hearts they released a word that **'Nothing that the white man is bringing will enter into this place'** As a result nothing of modernism ever entered, they were spiritually sealed or cut off from the community.

On hearing this information, he went on to God in deep repentance for his community and asked the Lord for direction on what to do. He was inspired by the Holy Spirit to go to the center of the town, run round the tree seven times and curse it. From that time on change came into the community. It was nothing but divine visitation through the mercies of the Lord:

> *'And after many days thou shalt be visited: in the latter years thou shalt come into the land that is brought back from the sword, and is gathered out of many people, against the mountains of Israel, which have been always waste:'* (Ezk. 38:8)

# Chapter 1 - GENERATION WASTERS.

1. Let the right hand of God move against the wasters of my generation in Jesus name.

2. Oh Lord! Cast out my inheritance out of his belly as you promised in Job 20:15.

3. I resist the foundation of evil transaction entered into on my behalf.

4. I receive fresh power, so that the generation wasters may not rob me of my inheritance.

5. I renounce and reject the operations of evil covenant of my fore fathers in Jesus name.

6. I forbid your operations in my family.

7. Let the territorial entities empowered by my community to affect my life be overthrown.

8. Every familiar entity is arrested by fire in Jesus name.

9. You ancestral wasters be dried up by the East Wind.

10. I receive strength to overcome them today.

# Chapter Two
# THE ROOT OF AFFLICTIONS

*'Although affliction cometh not forth of the dust, neither doth trouble spring out of the ground. Yet man is born unto trouble....'- Job 5:6-7*

## Introduction

Even though the affliction of life is so numerous in types and dimensions, yet they have their source most of the time in the devil. It is clear that every affliction has its root traceable to specific legal hold that the enemy has to afflict. Sometimes however, God brings judgment on people when they turn their back against His command. When the hedge is broken a serpent will always bite. This is because the wages of sin is death.

Without any doubt affliction does not just jump on people, it must have a reason to manifest. God's law does not permit injustice. This the devil and his agents know very well and so they draw their victim out of the hedge in order to afflict. In the book of Proverbs 26:2 it is written that *'...a curse causeless shall not alight.'*

Also in the book of Job in Chapter 5 verses 6-7 it is also confirmed that:

> *'Although affliction cometh not forth of the dust, neither doth trouble spring out of the ground. Yet man is born unto trouble....'-*

We read an interesting account of how the root of man's afflictions commenced in Genesis Chapter 3. It reveals how the Serpent tempted Eve and caused her to sin against God by eating the forbidden fruit. She in turn gave the same to her husband to eat in spite of God's warning. As a result of their disobedience to God's divine instruction, God put a curse upon them:

> *"... I will put enmity between thee and the woman, and between thy seed and her seed; it shall bruise thy head, and thou shalt bruise his heel"* (Gen. 3:15).

Here began a train of events that put man under the control of afflictions of life. From this point onwards man must sweat to eat, and the ground will yield for him thorns and thistles. The woman also had her own share of the curse:

## DEALING WITH GENERATION WASTERS

*'Unto the woman he said, I will greatly multiply thy sorrow and thy conception; in sorrow thou shalt bring forth children; and thy desire shall be to thy husband, and he shall rule over thee.'*

As soon as the devil heard God's words, he mapped out his strategy to destroy every male child in the line and Generation Wasters were on ground to achieve this plan.

These entities were willing tools in the hands of Satan to waste the lives of men. As a result he began to monitor any one that fits the picture he thought the seed of the woman should assume. In order to forestall its fulfillment, he moved against some sons of God who actually had nothing to do with the prophecy in order to stop them.

The undisputable manifestation of generation waster is clearly identified in the harvest of deaths, destructions and inexplicable material losses people experience in life. There is no limit to the level of destruction that this entity metes out to humanity. It can be so bad that a family can lose all its prominent sons in one year. The operations of generation wasters are without mercy. This enemy deploys spiritual weapons of mass destruction, hence living up to its name generation waster. A brief account of some of those he attacked is listed below.

### *i) Abel*
Having noted the fact that God accepted the sacrifice of Abel, he raised the spirit of envy, hate and murder

to rise up in Cain. Since he also saw some level of piety and love for God in Abel's conduct, he believed he was the seed of the woman. More so when Cain saw that Abel's sacrifice was accepted when his was not, he became livid with deadly anger. The devil motivated him to murder Abel through the influence of generation wasters and he executed the task with raw crudity. But Alas! The devil miscalculated, Abel was not that seed.

### ii) Lamech

When the devil realized his failure on Abel's murder he attacked many other folks along the line until he came to Lamech. He made a thorough mess of Lamech's life until he succeeded in making him to become the first polygamist and the second murderer:

> *'And Lamech said unto his wives, Adah and Zillah, Hear my voice; ye wives of Lamech, hearken unto my speech: for I have slain a man to my wounding, and a young man to my hurt'* (Gen. 4:23)

In his anguish of soul, Lamech described the punishment he deserved for his sin:

> *'If Cain shall be avenged sevenfold, truly Lamech seventy and seven fold'* (Gen. 4:25).

### iii) Seth

After this, a period of peace was experienced as Seth gave birth to Enos in Genesis 4:26 and the Bible declares that '..*then began men to call upon the name of the Lord'* What a wonderful departure from prayerlessness and failure? This man broke through the barriers or limitations of his time to bring forth a revival in prayer. Men's attention was diverted from idolatry unto the living God. Their blind eyes were open to the fact that they could call upon God and he would answer them.

### *iv) Enoch*

In the same spiritual framework we come to meet a wonderful friend of God called Enoch in Genesis 5:21. The Bible tells us in verse 22 that he walked with God, after he gave birth to Methusselah for three hundred years and he was caught up to be with the Lord. This man broke the chains of limitations that others before and after him suffered because he prayed. The bible through the revelation of the Holy Spirit gave a beautiful closing remark about him in Genesis 5:24

> *'And Enoch walked with God: and he was not; for God took him'*

### *v) Methusselah*

While the devil could not succeed in dealing with Enoch the man of prayer and friend of God, he took a pound of flesh from his son. We saw how the man was slowed down or limited in life through strategic attacks of the kingdom of darkness. What others achieved easily took him ages to accomplish. The Bible records how long it took him to have a son:

> *'And Methusselah lived an hundred eighty and seven years and begat Lamech'* (Gen 5:25).

Nothing significant was mentioned about him that he did for God. He came from the family of a prayer warrior, but nothing was said of him in this regards. While the Bible mentions the altars Abraham, Isaac, and Jacob raised for God, nothing of such was listed after his name. The only glaring achievement recorded after his name was that he '*..he begat sons and daughters'* (Gen 5:27). This means he was nothing but a baby factory pure and simple! The summary of his life is:

*"And all the days of Methusselah were nine hundred sixty and nine years: and he died"* (Gen 5:27).

There are people in this man's shoes. Their lives are filled with track records of unrestrained failure and reproach. The story is told of a man who suffered several disappointments in his bid to travel abroad in spite of obvious academic and financial advantages he possessed. While his failures lasted several decades, his breakthrough came at the age of seventy-two when he was given visa to travel abroad. This is what I call **'Methuselah miracle'**. What will this man achieve abroad at the age of seventy-two, when he should be preparing to answer the home call?

### *vi) Noah*
The battle against the seed of the woman reached its peak when Satan polluted the human race by causing angels to have sexual affairs with the daughters of men. As a result giants were brought into the world, hence affecting the course of events on the earth. God had

## DEALING WITH GENERATION WASTERS

to do a clean up exercise by wiping out the pollution through Noah's flood. Unfortunately after the flood, there was a brief respite and the situation on earth returned to business as usual. The devil moved Noah to plant a vineyard, get drunk, and put a curse on his son.

### *vii) Terah*

The story of Terah Abraham's father was the most pathetic. He made the man to turn back from his vision and chose his former life of idolatry. How do we know this? Let us trace these facts using his age and Abraham's as references. He gave birth to Abraham at the age of seventy (Gen. 11:26) and by the time Abraham left Ham at the age of seventy-five, (Gen. 12:4) Terah should be one hundred and forty-five. The Bible tells us in Acts 7:4 on the departures from Ur of Chaldees and Haran as described in Genesis thus:

> *'Then came he out of the land of the Chaldeans, and dwelt in Charran: and from thence, when his father was dead, God removed him into this land, wherein ye now dwell'.*

Looking closely at this verse one may be tempted to assume that there is a contradiction in it when placed beside the Genesis 12:4 account. There is no contradiction in God the verse only reveals the mind of God on what actually happened.

Let it be clear in your mind as earlier on mentioned that Terah was one hundred and forty-five when Abraham left Haran. Equally understand the fact that Abraham did not leave Haran willingly at the time he left, ***God removed him into this land, wherein ye now dwell'*** (Acts 7:4)

One may not be far from declaring that God forcefully removed him from Haran, in order to go fulfill the purpose of God for his life. Let us again draw your attention to another reason why God removed him from Haran. In the same verse of Scriptures we read '...***when his father was dead, God removed him into this land'*** Does this say anything to you? What it simply reveals is that God had to do a work of separation between Abraham and his father, Terah because the man had lost his spiritual cutting edge. In simple term he had died spiritually and in order not to affect his son Abraham for evil, there must be a separation.

Please recall that it was mentioned that he was one hundred and forty five when his son left him in Haran. He left Ur of Chaldees with the aim of getting to Canaan but he never got there because the evil works in the land influenced him. If the man was the age we claimed when Abraham left him, how old was he then when he physically died? Let us return to the book of Genesis to proffer answer to this question. In Genesis Chapter 11 verse 32 we read these words:

*"And the days of Terah were two hundred and five years: and Terah died in Haran"*

Now in simple arithmetic, when you take time to deduct his actual age of one hundred and forty-five, when Abraham left him at Haran, from his age of two hundred and five at death you are left with sixty. What

## DEALING WITH GENERATION WASTERS

did this man spend the rest sixty years of his life doing? Your guess is as good as ours he wasted it.

It may not be proper to leave the issue hanging; therefore what exactly did the man do for the rest sixty years of his life? Perhaps getting to the root of this subject matter may help you realize how easily a man can fall prey into the hands of generation wasters and waste his life without realizing it. Many today have spent the useful part of the lives roaming about without anything to show for it.

Now to the subject of discourse, let us closely examine the book of Joshua chapter 24 verse 2 for the answer. It reads:

*"..... Your fathers dwelt on the other side of the flood in old time, even Terah, the father of Abraham, and the father of Nachor: and they served other gods."*

We believe now that you have read the facts with your own eyes you will agree with us that there is no argument about the one in reference. In order to avoid any argument about whom Joshua was talking about, the Holy Spirit deliberately mentioned the name of his notable son, Abraham, and his other son Nachor. This should serve as a lesson to us that it is not the one that starts the race that receives the medal, but he that finishes the race by enduring to the end. Hence, Terah, the father of Abraham ended the race very badly, serving other gods and lost everything he had to the devil.

## *viii) Elimelech*

In some cases it may be the disobedience of the ancestral fathers to God's commandments that open up the family to ancestral affliction. This we see in the life of Elimelech and his children in the book of Ruth 1:1-5, 20-22. He died and his children died in quick succession in the land of Moab. His generation was completely wiped out because he ran out of God's covering to a strange land.

## *ix) Judah*

The same is true of Judah in Gen 38 who married a Canaanitish woman in spite of God's warning. The evil spirit of wickedness manifested in both of them and God killed them. Even though the Bible did not tell us what the first son did to be called wicked, the second son wasted the 'seed' by spilling it to the ground in order not to raise an offspring for his brother:

> *'An Onan knew that the seed should not be his; and it came to pass, when he went in unto his brother's wife, that he spilled it on the ground, lest he should give seed to his brother. And the thing which he did displeased the Lord wherefore he slew him also'* (Gen 38:9-11)

The quick demise of his two sons forced him to hide the third called Shelah and advised the daughter in law to remain in her father's house until the boy be grown up. However, in Tamar's desperation she planned a coup for her father in law and the man fell for the trick because he was sexually weak. As a result of the sexual relationship that took place a curse of the law came into operation:

> *'A bastard shall not enter into the congregation of the Lord; even to his tenth generation shall he not enter...'* (Deut. 23:2)

This caused the delay of the royal lineage from becoming kings for nine generations until David mounted the throne. This was because a bastard could not be reckoned with in the king's lineage. The ascension of David to the throne prepared the way for the restoration of the lineage of Christ.

We need to be wary of worldly attraction and the way we easily get carried away. We must have great expectations, because this is the only way to make it to the end. Abraham, Isaac, Jacob, the twelve patriarchs and David were also not spared in the manhunt for the seed of the woman. Each had his own share of the temptations to discredit them and make them unfit for the roles he thought they were to assume. But we thank God for his mercies who makes all things well in his time.

## *Reasons for oppression*

There are several reasons that may cause the loopholes of oppressions under review. Some of these are listed to help us identify reasons why the enemy legally afflicts.

## i) Idolatry

In the case of Abraham's lineage, it was simply **idolatry** and the Bible reveals to us that

> *'He that breaketh the edge a serpent will bite'* (Eccl 10:8).

When generation wasters manifest it always end in death and destruction. A good reference point to the destructive influence of idolatry is mentioned in Jeremiah 48:13 where the bible hints us that

> *"...the house of Israel was ashamed of Bethel their confidence".*

When was Bethel the confidence of Israel? This was when Jeroboam built two golden calves – one in Bethel and the other in Dan. He did this to discourage the people from going to Jerusalem to worship, because he was afraid he might lose them:

> *'And Jeroboam, said in his heart, Now shall the kingdom return to the house of David. If this people go up to do sacrifice in Jerusalem....'* (I Kings 12:26-27).

These calves he had raised not only became a lie to the people, but also a sin. The people went to worship before idols that they gave the glory of God to the creation of their own hands:

> *'...behold thy gods, O Israel, which brought thee up out of the land of Egypt'* (v28).

## DEALING WITH GENERATION WASTERS

This man dissuaded the people from worshipping God in the proper manner. The manner and mode of worship simply differed from God's ordained pattern. He made himself priests of the lowest of the people and made a mockery of priesthood. The timing ordained by God was not only altered, but also ran the worship according to the dictate of his heart as recorded in .I Kings 12:23

*'So he offered upon the altar which he had made in Bethel the fifteenth day of the eight month, even in the month which, even in the month which he had devised of his own heart: and ordained a feast unto the children of Israel: and he offered upon the altar, and burnt incense.'*

It is important to mention that God hates rebellion and pride. He resists the proud from afar off and just cannot stand them. The same treatment of sending wandering spirit that caused Moab to wander was pronounced on Israel in Numbers 14 verse 33:

*"And your children shall wander in the wilderness forty years, and bear your whoredoms, until your carcases be wasted in the wilderness."*

One significant thing observed in this scripture is the fact that the wandering spirit has an able deadly associate called *the generation waster*. In order to fulfill God's pronouncement upon them, the wandering spirit kept them going in circles for upward of thirty-eight years until they were all *'..wasted in the wilderness'*:

> *"And the space in which we came from Kadesh-barnea, until we were come over the brook Zered, was thirty and eight years; until all the generation of the men of war were wasted out from among the host, as the Lord sware unto them."* (Deut. 2:14).

### ii) Disobedience

Another cause is **disobedience** to God's divine instructions. He that hath ear let him hear is the counsel of the Lord. We are also warned in Is. 42:23:

> *'Who among you will give ear to this? Who will hearken and hear for the time to come?'*

What are they to give ear to? God's divine instruction that should keep them from evil, if they diligent walk in his ways. But they would not and therefore God had a case against them as he declared in the same book of Isaiah in verse 24:

> *Who gave Jacob for a spoil, and Israel to the robbers? Did not the Lord, he against whom we have sinned? For they would not walk in his ways, neither were they obedient unto his law.*

## *iii)* **Ignorance**

Ignorance also stood out as a sore thumb in the problem, and it enabled them to fall into satanic traps. God in his raw anger moved against him and

> *'...poured upon him the fury of his anger, and the strength of battle: and it hath set him on fire round about, yet he knew not: and it burned him, yet he laid it not to heart'* (Is 42:25)

A man that God has moved against and does not know is a dead man. Who can hear his appeal, except God shows him mercy? Some today are going through God's raw dealings yet they keep binding the devil. May God open such eyes, help them to repent and cry for His mercy.

The most pathetic of manifestation of generation wasters is recorded in Mt 22:25-27 where seven sons of a family died without leaving any seed behind. In spite of all the efforts made to produce seed, everything proved abortive and everyone died to the bargain. The woman became a slaughter slab to each of the men that had her. At the end she herself died.

I remember a testimony given by a pastor friend of a woman that lost several husbands each time she had her fourth child. In each instance, as soon as the husband dies, all the four children will begin to die within a space of one year without remedy. It was when she was on her fourth husband and thirteen out of sixteen children had died that she realized the regular cycle of death and cried out for help. The church she ran to, took up her case, and interceded for God's mercy to spare the lives of her last three children and God heard their cry for mercy.

### *iv)* **Reneging on promises**
Reneging on promises made to a small god or goddess that the ancestors worship was another reason for oppression. The very terrible one is when men turn their backs at the living God. The consequence of this is very grave.

We see clear examples in the book of Joel how resources were wasted and men could not enjoy their God given inheritances. The attack was so much that the drunkards were challenged to wake up and weep because the new wine was cut off from their mouth. The people were advised to lament like a virgin crying for the loss of the husband of her youth. Even the priests, the ministers of God, the husbandmen and vinedressers were all affected in this terrible draught. The gory details revealed in the book of Joel is frightening:

> *'The field is wasted, the land mourneth; for the corn is wasted: the new wine is dried up, the oil languisheth. The seed is rotten under their clods, the garners are laid desolate, the barns are broken down; for the corn is withered.*
>
> *How do the beasts groan! The herds of cattle are perplexed, because they have no pasture; yea, the flocks of sheep are made desolate.'*
> (Joel 1:10,17-18).

## DEALING WITH GENERATION WASTERS

While the situation persisted, the people seemed hopeless and helpless. Even the priests did not know what to do. It was a season of unrestrained disaster and calamity became the order of the day. In short it was a season of despair everywhere. We thank God that in crisis our Lord never forsake us and always makes a way where their seem to be no way. Through the mercies of God it was revealed that it was a time for the priest to buckle up

> *'... and lament,.....: howl, ye ministers of the altar: come lie all night in sackcloth, ye ministers of my God: for the meat offering and the drink offering is witholden from the house of your God. Sanctify ye a fast, call a solemn assembly, gather the elders and all the inheritance of the land into the house of the Lord your God, and cry unto the Lord.'* (Joel 1:13-14)

### v) Foxes on desolate (prayer) mountains

Prayerlessness or Foxes on desolate (prayer) mountains is another cause of oppression. Ordinarily foxes do not walk upon mountains in impunity because they know that men may appear at any time to challenge their audacity. Yet we see something to the contrary in the way some of us carelessly carry on. There seems to be an emptiness, a vacuum and absence of dominion in the place of prayer:

> *"Because of the mountain of Zion, which is desolate the foxes walk upon it."* (Lam. 5:18)

The reason why foxes walk upon the mountain of Zion, which by interpretation is the mountain of prayer, is because men abandoned their duty posts. They left a vibrant place of warfare so desolate that foxes had field day and took total control of the place of generating power. Tremendous power is only made available in the place of prayer. The amplified version of James 5:16 confirms this:

***'..The earnest (heartfelt continued) prayer of a righteous man makes tremendous power available – dynamic in its working'***

Foxes represent evil men operating easily in the midst of God's people. They are men without scruples who operate with utmost wickedness. The Bible in Psalm 14 verse 4 refers to them as workers of iniquity who have no knowledge but ***"…eat up my people as they eat bread and call not upon God"***

Since power had been given to them on the platter of gold, by the abdication of our responsibility, they have totally brought corruption to some work in the vineyard. Hopes and aspirations have been dashed. Many rising stars have been cut off from their destinies. Our beautiful ones have been lied to and their treasures vandalized, while we turn our faces the other way.

The vineyard itself has been so damaged that strange men tread where angels dare not, while we watch our inheritance being carted away. We have come to that climax where in Songs of Solomon the writer cannot help but cry in Chapter 2 verse 15: ***"Take us the foxes, the little foxes, that spoil the vine:…"***

These little foxes are character traits that in themselves so insignificant but when they grow would bring destruction or death to the person. These are the *"... little leaven that leavenneth the whole lump"*. (I Cor. 5:6)

## *Purge Yourself From The Old Leaven*

Where this is the situation we need to purge our selves of the *"old leaven"* in order to be right with God. When we are full of ourselves we are courting disaster, and deliberately having fellowship with untimely destruction. It is a sign of deathly ease that results in belated regrets. The person that is arrogant, proud or full of himself is like Moab that *".. hath been at ease from his youth,.."* (Jer. 48:11).

This is a state of flippant abuse, wantonness, and arrogance. Such a person had never faced serious challenges in life, and having gotten no experiential knowledge of situations around him, and so he takes many things for granted. He toys easily with serious spiritual conditions and downplays it to ridiculous level. This is simply because: *"....he hath settled on his lees,.."*

Being settled on the lees is a state whereby dirt settles under water or any liquid content. It only comes up when stirred up. It is a terrible mixture that changes the state of the water or liquid content. Therefore, in order for the water or liquid content to maintain its perfect state it must be *"... emptied from vessel to vessel,...".*

Sometimes certain experiences in life, which leave us helpless and hopeless until God intervenes, assist us in redefining our philosophy in life and bring about forceful change. While this problem persists, we experience captivity or limitation and are hindered from making progress in life. Sometimes this may be the only way to get somebody's attention, assist them to perceive godly things and by so doing force a change in character.

The Bible in fact points to these salient observations when talking about the attitude or character of Moab to his personal life. The reason advanced for his misconduct is that because he:

*"....hath not been emptied from vessel to vessel, neither hath he gone into captivity: therefore his taste remained in him, and his scent is not changed."* (Jer. 48:11).

It is about time the warning of God was heeded or God himself will bring about a forceful change. We have seen this happen in his word and the rebellious this time around shall not be an exception because God:

*"...will send unto him wanderers, that shall cause him to wander, and shall empty his vessels, and break their bottles."* (Jer. 48:12).

When God personally supervises a man's punishment, the man has no hope but to look up to God for mercy.

The end result is that the person will be ashamed just as Moab was ashamed of its idol (Chemosh) and *"... as the house of Israel was ashamed of Bethel their confidence."* (Jer. 48:13).

# Chapter 2 – THE ROOT OF AFFLICTIONS

1. In the name of Jesus, lift up your heads, O ye gates; and be ye lift up, ye everlasting doors.

2. I come against the inner caucus of evil men, working against my progress in Jesus name.

3. I repent, reject and renounce any unknown covenants binding my family to poverty and failure.

4. I command fire and brimstone to fall upon the priest and the altar of evil sacrifice raised against me.

5. I release fire and brimstone upon every covenant enforcer, limiting my lineage from going forward.

6. I command every gate shut against my family to be opened now in Jesus name.

7. I neutralize all unknown agreement between my village, town or city with satanic gatekeepers in Jesus name.

8. I resist every legal ground that my ancestors had given satanic powers to rule my lineage. I proclaim the Lordship of Jesus over my family and I.

9. O Lord! Let my people who sit in darkness see the great slight and gravitate towards liberty in Jesus name.

10. O Lord, expose every ploy of Satan to bind me in ignorance in Jesus name.

# Chapter Three
# THE OPERATIONS OF GENERATION WASTERS?

*'....I created the waster to destroy.' - Isaiah 54:16*

## *Introduction*

As mentioned in the previous chapter, the generation wasters are satanic entities that consistently operate with unbroken coalition with spiritual gates. These are demonic entities that are known only for wasting the lives of generations of people. They visit with impunity, a family lineage, with similar afflictions down the generation. In their operations, they ensure that such generations battle with inherited curses and afflictions that result in the early termination of their lives.

Several generations down the line are under the clutches of entities of darkness against their will. It is sad to mention that many do not know the source of their problems and why they have to go through it. All they have come to identify with, in all these, is the similarity in the afflictions down the generation.

Also the fact that, in spite of several precautionary measures that the human knowledge could proffer in order not to suffer untimely death, they still die inexplicably. Some even succumb to sacrifices and offerings prescribed by the ancestral overlords, in order to appease the gods that they may live, yet the long hand of the destroyer still catches up with them. As a result of their sordid experiences, hopelessness and despair have become their close associates.

It is at this point that some begin to think that the way out of the affliction is to run away to another community or country. When they successfully do so, they later discover that their time of respite was just for a while, as the same problem begins to rear up its ugly head where they now live.

What usually happens is that these spirits pass their victims case files to wherever they go and the ruling spirits in the territory take over the ministry of afflictions. Why this is possible is because, every transaction between the fathers and the kingdom of darkness are recorded and filed away till it is needed for execution.

Hence the solution is not in running away but waiting to confront them. It is important to ask questions, make crucial observations and take the appropriate spiritual decision to halt the destroyer of the generations. This is not only wise but also necessary for one to be able to fulfill one's God-given destiny in Christ.

## *Strongholds Of Affliction*

In order to confront the powers of darkness, one must know their modus operandi. In addition, one needs to know some of the operational tricks they play to bring their victims under total subjection. These are the strongholds or legal grounds that give them authority and the audacity to plunder men's lives or destinies. All these are briefly itemized below for one to be able to draw one's conclusions and take appropriate actions as the Holy Spirit permits.

### *i) The sins of the fathers*
As mentioned earlier, every transaction the fathers had with the spirits are filed away till it is needed for execution. When the time to effect the terms of the contract or transaction is up, the monitoring spirits will be on the look out for compliance. Both the covenant tokens, covenant terms and covenant responsibilities are diligently monitored. Where these are done, there will be no problem at all. But where there is a default either by the one who entered into the contract or his children, covenant enforcers will viciously move in against the recalcitrant and helpless victim.

They capitalize on the sins of the fathers to afflict, and in effecting this, they rely solely on the spiritual documents in their possession for the legality to afflict. These documents are reference points to the transactions the fore fathers entered into on behalf of their children born or unborn. These are the activities of the past, the promises made, and responsibilities tied to them. Being ignorant of them is what gives the devil the opportunity to afflict with impunity. This is graphically expressed in the book of Lamentation in Chapter 5:17:

> *'Our fathers have sinned, and are not; and we have borne their iniquities.'*

As long as those covenants are still standing the victim remains a prey. That is why it is very important to inquire, repent, renounce, and reject all known and unknown covenants or evil transactions entered into by the ancestors on one's behalf.

The generation wasters have, through this method, put the generations born and unborn into perpetual bondage, because of the sins of the fathers. They ensure that the generation they start dealing with pays the backlog of tokens denied them over the years. In a situation like this, it is usually difficult to know the root of the problem, except through revelation. This is the only way the victim is able to know what to do to be free.

Where you are born into cannot be your choice, it is God that decides that. But unfortunately some have been born into a family deeply rooted in trouble as Job 5:6-7 confirms:

*'Although affliction cometh not forth of the dust, neither doth trouble spring out of the ground; yet man is born unto trouble,......'*

The sins of the fathers have caused trouble for many families and have made them to become lawful captives. The sins have made them to enjoy evil relationship with entities of darkness but unknown to them the consequences are grievous. In Psalms 97:7 it is written that:

*'Confounded be all they that serve graven images, that boast themselves of idols....'*

Hence, no matter where they run, they will remain perpetual victim of failure, disappointment, and embarrassment except they do something about it. We have seen the generation wasters in operation in various parts of the Bible. Their operations have always been known to be very ruthless and without mercy. In short, their specific assignment is to steal, kill and destroy.

### ii) They receive judgment against their victim

The generation wasters receive judgment against people and like bailiffs go out to enforce it. They operate better in a situation where their victim does not know the odds against him. They thrive easily in an atmosphere where ignorance is exalted; hypocrisy is enthroned and coroneted with the crown of foolishness. Since more often than not the situation is organized to look hopeless, the victim usually resigns to fate and believes that one day the Lord will do it. In extreme cases they believe it is a cross that God has chosen for their family to bear.

This obvious ignorance gives the powers greater latitude to deal with their victim. All that God expects one to do in situation like this is to *'Submit ….to God. Resist the devil, and he will flee from you.'* (Jas 4:7).

The secret behind the suffering of Israel is revealed in the book of Zephaniah in Chapter 3 verses 14 to 15. The enemy pummeled the nation and her king to submission, yet they knew not the root of their problems. The Lord had to intervene by going directly after the root. The daughters were told to sing, since they had not been singing because of the problems before them. The people were told to shout the shout of victory because God had moved against their enemy. They were told to *'…be glad and rejoice with all the heart,..'* Why? God normally does this to find out where our trust lies. He always desires that we rejoice even before we know or see the miracles he had wrath.

However, Verse 15 of the book in focus tells us that: *'The Lord hath taken away thy judgments..'.* This was what gave legality to the enemy. As long as the judgment is standing every resistance will be faulted and indeed equally fail.

The issue of judgment had been sorted out in the book of Romans Chapter 8:1:

> *'There is therefore now no more condemnation to them which are in Christ Jesus, who walk not after the flesh, but after the spirit.'*

## DEALING WITH GENERATION WASTERS

As long as the flesh is allowed to rule there will still be condemnation. Having sorted out this, he moved against the enemy and made a show of them openly. He thereafter declared that I the Lord *'...hath cast out thine enemy:'* (v15)

With this truth made available, he ensured that all the wickedness of the enemy was silenced for good. He equally made sure that his goodness and mercies should not depart from his people. Why? This is because *'.. the king of Israel, even the Lord, is in the midst of thee...'* (v15). Therefore you will enjoy divine protection. The mountains will surround you as it surrounds Jerusalem. Your labor will endure and will not sow for trouble. He crowned it with the fact that, I have dealt with the enemy therefore, *'..thou shalt not see evil any more.'* (v15)

### iii) They Accuse

It is indeed the facts of scriptures that one of the things the devil knows how to do best is his role of the accuser of the brethren. Since, he assumed this role he has never rested as the Bible confirms in the book of Job Chapter 1 verse 7. In answer to God's probing question on where he was coming from:

> *'Then Satan answered the Lord, and said, From going to and fro in the earth, and from walking up and down in it.'* (Job 1:7).

Hardly did God finish talking about Job that he began to accuse him before God. *'..... Doth Job fear God for nought?'* (v9). Have you not made provisions to promote and protect him? You put forth your hand on all that he has; he will curse you to your face. He went on until God said:

> *'..Behold, all that he hath is in thy power; only upon himself put not forth thine hand...'*

He went away immediately from God's presence and Jobs nightmares started.

Two significant refrains are noted in the attacks that Satan launched against Job. The first refrain noticed after a messenger came to Job, is:

> *'While he was yet speaking, there came also another...'* (references- v16, 17 and 18).

The second is:

> *'....and I only am escaped alone to tell thee.'* (v15, 16, 17, and 19).

The close marking Satan gave Job was a clear evidence of taking an advantage of the opportunity given him to attack. He indeed deliberately left a witness behind to cause lasting pains for him as the accounts of the disaster were been rendered to him. He thought he could break Job, but in it all he maintained his testimony before God and:

> *'...the accuser of our brethren is cast down, which accused them before our God day and night.'* (Rev 12:10).

## *DEALING WITH GENERATION WASTERS*

Who ever the spirit of generation waster influences is always a vicious, deadly, and unforgiving fellow. They always watch out for a person's human frailty to use against him and are very critical of others to the point of death. The story of Jesus' encounter with the man with the withered hand and the Pharisees is a good case in point. Here was a man who needed help, but the Bible tells us that *'...they watched him, whether he would heal him on a Sabbath day;....'*

They kept watch because they knew that Jesus had one passion, and that is he could not watch a man suffer Sabbath or no Sabbath. Hence, they fastened their eyes on his every move so *'...that they might accuse him'* like their father Satan would have done. He being the wisdom of God knew what to do. He commanded the sick man to stand up. Then he turned to his accusers and said:

*'...Is it lawful to do good on the Sabbath days, or to do evil? To save life or to kill?'* (v4)

Here the Lord Jesus asked many questions in one. He indeed pulled the carpets under their feet and had no answer for his questions. They shut their mouth momentarily, while their heart was working out the next evil action to take.

Can you comprehend the fact that they could not match Jesus' question of doing good with the right actions. All the while they are men who stick simply to the rules no matter how tough it is. They do not bend even if mercy is required. Hence, they:

> *'...went forth, and straightway took counsel with the Herodians against him, how they might destroy him.'* (v6)

That is generation wasters for you – Sabbath or no Sabbath, evil and death are their portions.

### iv) They Seduce

They seduce men to commit sin in order to make them prone to spirit of destruction and thereby waste their generation. Evil counselors are always on hand to bring forward the counsel that will lead to destruction. The case of King Ahaziah is a ready reference here. In II Chronicles 21:3 we are told that:

> *'He also walked in the ways of the house of Ahab: for his mother was his counselor to do wickedly.'*

When one is seduced to do evil the ultimate end is destruction. The king was foolish enough to listen to wrong counsel and therefore did evil in the sight of God. He was compared with the house of Ahab in evil deeds. This was no surprise as the Bible tells us in verse 4 that:

> *'....they were his counselors after the death of his father to destruction'*

His destruction, which was of God, eventual came when Jehu was executing judgment upon the house of Ahab. Ahaziah went out with Jehoram against Jehu that God had appointed and anointed to deal with the house

## DEALING WITH GENERATION WASTERS

of Ahab. While dealing with Ahab's house he found the princes of Judah and brethren of Ahaziah, among the company and he killed them. He thereafter:

*'...sought Ahaziah and they caught him, (for he was hid in Samaria,) and brought him to Jehu: and when they had slain him, they buried him....'* (v9)

This man died in a cause that did not concern him because, he dared to walk in wrong company and had evil communication with evil men.

### v) They induce fear

They operate based on induced fear that has its origin in indoctrination. Sometimes it may be the fear of how my tomorrow would be. I better begin to make plans and some times such plans are not clean ones. Satanic ideas begin to infiltrate the thoughts of a once righteous man. He begins to believe the lie that says **'Heavens help those who help themselves'**.

The servant of Elisha, Gehazi, fell into this trap, and collected the last bit of worldly riches he was to amass as the servant of the prophet. He was satanically convinced that his master must have been a fool to have spared Naaman with his riches. He therefore quickly thought up a foolproof plan, so he probably must have thought, to collect his portion from him.

*'But Gehazi, the servant of Elisha the man of God, said, behold, my master hath spared Naaman this Syrian, in not receiving at his*

*hands that which he brought: but, as the Lord liveth, I will run after him, and take somewhat of him.'* (II Kings 5:20).

He followed up these thoughts with rapid response action and indeed took more than he bargained for because Naaman was a generous man. He was also a man that appreciates people and believed that God would heal him, and therefore did not come empty handed. He was loaded with gifts and was willing to part with as many of the gifts he brought. But alas they were leprous gifts!

After collecting his gifts and hiding them in the house the Bible tells us after the men departed:

*'But he went in, and stood before his master. And Elisha said unto him, Whence comest thou, Gehazi? And he said, Thy servant went no wither.*

*And he said unto him, Went not mine heart with thee, when the man turned again from his chariot to meet thee? Is it time to receive money, and to receive garments, and oliveyards, and oxen, and menservants, and maidservants?*

*The leprousy therefore of Naaman shall cleave unto thee, and unto thy seed for ever. And he went out from his presence a leper as white as snow.'* (II Kings 5:25-27)

## DEALING WITH GENERATION WASTERS

There is time for everything, a time to receive gifts and a time to refuse it, but Gehazi has no qualms. He was a toll collector general. Nobody escaped his notice. Therefore due to greed and avarice, he collected leprous gifts and procured generations of leprosy for himself and his generations born and unborn. Servants of powerful men of God beware!

### *vi) They intimidate, manipulate, and dominate*
They begin to intimidate a man, after inducing him through fear, with facts at their disposals in order to derail him from his focus. When the enemy saw that they could not derail Jesus from his vision they raised opposition from among circle of friends. The Lord Jesus was holding a meeting in which: *'...the multitude cometh together -again, so that they could not so much as eat bread.'* (Mk 3:21)

Furthermore, the Bible tells us that, on hearing this his friends:

> *'....went out to lay hold on him: for they said, He is beside himself'* (v21).

The Lord however refused to be intimidated. Yet his friends might not have known it, they were under the manipulation and domination of Satan as instruments of derailment of focus in executing a God-given vision. When this failed, the enemy struck again with evil reports against him. In verse 22 we are told that the scribes who came down all the way from Jerusalem claimed that:

> *'..He hath Beelzebub, and by the prince of the devils casteth he out devils.'*

As expected through divine wisdom he silenced them and killed every attempt to intimidate him to submission and derail his focus on his vision to save humanity from the oppression of Satan.

One true thing about the devil is that he is a stubborn fellow and never gives up so easily. When he saw that the second attempt had failed to derail Jesus from his vision, he deployed another missile against him. In the same Chapter in verse 31, he raised a formidable distraction from among his home.

> *'There came then his brethren and his mother, and, standing without, sent unto him, calling him.'*

At such a crucial time when he was delivering his Father's message to the lost, that was when they came looking for him.

He knew the game plan of the enemy too well. Now what was happening as mentioned earlier was a simple case of manipulation and domination in respect of his friends, the scribes and the members of his family. Being a familiar terrain the Lord Jesus gave an answer that knocked the ground out of their feet:

> *'And he answered them, saying, who is my mother, or my brethren?*

*And he looked round about on them which sat about him, and said, Behold my mother and my brethren!*

*For whosoever shall do the will of God, the same is my brother, and my sister, and mother.'* (v33-35).

The last statement revealed at that point in time where his brethren and mother stood on the account of God's will and Jesus' vision. They were as verse 31 tells us *'…. standing without…'* and did not measure up in God's eyes as faithful laborers together with him. If they were with Jesus, they ought to have been inside not *'without'*. Hence, the reason they became easy prey for indoctrination, intimidation, manipulation and domination.

### vii) Death or Destruction is their goal

The Psalm of David in Chapter 137:7-9 reveal to us the wickedness of Edom and how they viciously destroyed the people of God. They carried out operation no mercy and the prayer of the Psalmist was for God to:

*'Remember….the children of Edom in the day of Jerusalem; who said, Rase it, rase it, even to the foundation thereof.'* (Ps 137:7).

Even the daughter of Babylon was involved, and hence they were supposed to be destroyed. Happy should be the one *'..that rewardeth thee as thou hast served us.'* (Ps 137:8). How did these wicked people serve the people of God? They ripped open the bellies of the pregnant women and *'...dasheth (their) little ones against the stones.'* (Ps 137:9)

Whoever this wicked spirit possesses is under the worst influence of death and destruction the world could not have ever imagined. The book of Esther helps one to have an insight into this, when one reflects on the matter of Haman versus Mordecai. A domestic problem was elevated into national focus, and was given so much attention that the financial drive to achieve solution was too enormous to comprehend.

When Haman saw that Mordecai neither bowed nor reverenced him, he became desperately angry and was filled with murderous rage. One may not be wrong to claim that he was filled with the spirit of destruction and murder. This is because the Bible tells us that he *'..was...full of wrath'*, just like a man can be filled of the spirit. In Haman's case, it was an in filling of unholy spirit, as we saw also manifested in the people that effected the killing of Stephen in Acts of the Apostles.

*'Then they cried out with a loud voice; and stopped their ears, and ran upon him with one accord, And cast him out of the city, and stoned him;.....'* (Acts 7:57-58)

From the moment of his possession, he considered it and insult to kill Modecai alone, therefore he: *'...sought to destroy all the Jews that were throughout the whole kingdom...'* (Est. 3:6).

This reveals the reason behind the senseless passion that overrides those possessed by the spirit called

# Chapter Four
# MANIFESTATIONS OF GENERATION WASTERS

*'...Because of the mountain of Zion, which is desolate the foxes walk upon it."- Lam 5:18*

## *Introduction*

The manifestations of generation wasters are clearly evident in the lives of some families, but because of ignorance, they are not aware of this satanic condition. Sometimes the deed of destructions would have been concluded, before they realize what is happening. In some situation even when they are knowledgeable enough to identify the prevailing problem, they keep it to themselves to handle it alone.

It is erroneously believed that keeping it in the family will save them from unnecessary embarrassment. So they usually will not cry out until it gets out of hands.

This gives the enemy undue advantage and more than enough time to 'waste' such families.

In addition, the reliance of some families on traditional healers or fetish priests has placed them in the hands of agents of the devil who without any doubt know what they are confronting, but dare not tell them. Sometimes the forces involved are so deadly that they warn the fetish priests not to meddle in the affairs that did not concern them or pay dearly for it. This priest, not desiring to risk his life to confront them, play along with the victim in pretence, until he gets fed up and goes.

There now begins a journey into futility, as he keeps knocking frantically on all kind of doors until he meets with the mercy of God. Somehow God has a way of leading men towards him in a spectacular encounter. It is at this point that the root of ignorance is destroyed and men are set free from bondage. The blessings that follow are better experienced than imagined.

For examples, the catalogue of abuses, torments, harassments, embarrassments, and humiliations experienced in the course of seeking for deliverance is wiped off through God's abundant mercies. Hopelessness and despair are also overcome because the light is come into the present darkness being experienced. The barriers raised to cause untimely death or destruction are pulled down.

Because they exist is the reason why members of some families have not been able to outlive certain age, successfully build houses, buy cars, succeed in business or even produce a graduate. The moment they cross this barrier they either go insane, suddenly disappear into oblivion, die or an inexplicable misfortune happens to them. It is always a case of no win situation, because the spiritual time bomb set must leave a deadly mark behind. The exception in this scenario is if Jesus is in the picture.

## *Generation of Carelessness*

The problems some face in life have come down the generation without showing neither degree of concern nor hope of redress. So many things have been taken for granted and men carry on as if it is business as usual. They relax while their enemy is at work monitoring their every move in order to know when to strike.

Even though the trend is always the same down the line, some people's minds have become so warped that they cannot think straight and identify this obvious recurrence. And when you point this out to them, they always find ready-made reasons to explain it away. When further pressure is mounted on them, they believe you have either become superstitious or mischievous. At the extreme they tag you a fanatic who sees demons in everything.

The essential truth about it all is that many are not sensitive in their spirit. Things have degenerated so badly that we dine with the devil and yet do not know it. We welcome with open hands enemies (serpents) into our homes and shut out friends (doves) who continue to vehemently cry about the error of our judgment and the disaster that is about to strike.

We need God to open our eyes as well as give us insight into things we do not understand. These can only be attained through consistent praying, but many have become so weak in the place of prayer.

Where opportunities arise for us to sort out the limitations in our lives, some procrastinate and carelessly trade away their future at the altar of seeking for affluence. The time that ought to be spent in wailing prayers is substituted with pursuing hard currency, and hence the enemy is left to rule in impunity. Lives are snuffed out at the whims and caprices of the oppressor. Careless living is costly. Correcting the damage it elicits is an uphill task and is sometimes irreparable. We must therefore watch and pray.

### *a) The Elders of Gadara*
The generation of carelessness always easily brings to mind the story of the Elders of Gadara. That is their reaction to the work of deliverance wrath by the Lord Jesus Christ on the mad man of Gadara. The outcome of the deliverance is a good reference to the manipulation of the territorial spirit at work in the lives of ignorant victims. Without mincing words, the territorial powers terribly arrested the elders that they all spoke with one voice against the good deed Jesus did.

When men operate under the influence of unseen forces of darkness, whether their action stands to good reason really does not matter Their conviction in cases

## DEALING WITH GENERATION WASTERS

like this is so strong that they believe their reactions actually come out of their own volition, but the truth is that they are under controlling influences of satanic entities. It will take the grace of God to open the eyes of such men.

Examining the case of the mad man for example, may open our eyes to some basic truths in the operations of wicked forces. Here was a man who had his dwelling among the tombs and no man had succeeded in keeping him bound with chains. This man had messed many men up and the Bible also confirmed that *'..neither could any man tame him'* (Mk 5:4).

He had become a public nuisance and a thorn in the flesh of the community. The violent or vicious spirits manifesting through him kept him awake day and night, crying and cutting himself. This alone in itself should arouse pity or compassion in those who saw him suffer hopelessly and helplessly. Yet the elders were not moved, but were more concerned with the loss of their swine and the need to get rid of Jesus from their community.

The demons knew their time had come and tried every means to secure their position. They tried to use the last tricks in their arsenals to stop the Lord Jesus at all cost from delivering the man. So when the demoniac saw the king of kings and the Lord of Lords, *'..afar off, he ran and worshipped him'* (Mk 5:6). This was the demon's first trick (worshipping the Lord) to disarm him from releasing his superior firepower that will culminate in the mad man's deliverance.

Secondly, the demons spoke through the mad man and causing him to cry with a loud voice,

> *'What have I to with thee Jesus thou son of the most high God?'* (Mk 5:7).

They thought this could intimidate the Lord Jesus: If one does not know the history of the tribe of Gad, the direct assault of satanic entities through the mad man may not make meaning to one.

Why did he speak to the Lord Jesus in this manner? It was because the territorial powers had a legal reason to operate in that territory and the people wanted it so. The power was in essence saying **'Jesus what is your business in this legitimate dominion that I am enjoying here'.**

### b) *The tribe of Gad*

Let us now examine the background story for clearer understanding of the history of the tribe of Gad. The Bible reveals that the tribe of Reuben and Gad had *'..a very great multitude of cattle'* (Num 32:1). When they saw that the lands of Jazer and Gilead were good for rearing cattle they were seductively attracted to them. This was the lust of the eye in manifestation. Hence they went to Moses and the princes of the congregation in Num 32:4-5 saying:

> *'..the country which the Lord smote before the congregation of Israel, is a land for cattle, and thy servants have cattle;*

## DEALING WITH GENERATION WASTERS

***Wherefore, said they, if we have found grace in thy sight, let this land be given unto thy servants for a possession, and bring us not over Jordan.'***

Through this seduction and deceit, they fell for Satan's ploy to waste their generation. They chose the option of staying back at the other side of Jordan to rear cattle in spite of Moses' initial objection to their decision. However, after much persuasion they agreed to go with the other tribes to fight and return to the land they believed was good to rear cattle. Thereafter Moses allowed them to inherit the land east of Jordan.

What connection has Gad with Gadara? The Nelson's New Illustrated Bible Dictionary throws more light on the fact that **'..The territory of Gad lay east of the Jordan River...'** pg 467. The same dictionary while referring to the city the mad man of Gadara was encountered describes the city of Gadarenes as **'..The city (that) was on the east side of Jordan River,...'** pg 468.

Further more Dakes Annotated Reference Bible referring to Mk 5:1 reference 'e' pg 39 hints that **'Gadara was a city south of the sea of Galilee and east of Jordan....'** . This in essence confirms that the tribe of Gad and the people of Gadara are the same as seen in the gospel of Mark.

## The Territorial Power over Gad

Having laid this necessary and very important foundation, let us see how territorial powers blinded generations of people misguided and misled them into organized destruction. Hence the territorial spirit was on legitimate ground when in Mk 5:12 he deployed his third trick and

> *'..besought him saying, Send us into the swine, that we may enter into them.'*

Notice the Bible says *'And all the devils..'* and the Legion himself stated in verse 9 that *'..we are many'*. Why did Jesus answer this unusual prayer, for it is only in this place that he allowed demons to dictate to him? He did it to show his displeasure to the actions of Reuben and Gad in staying back at the other side of Jordan. They backslid so much that they moved away from rearing cattle to rearing swine!

That the demons had lien with the people is not a thing to contest because the Bible declares that *'..he besought him that he would not send them away out of the country'* (Mk 5:10). The demons loved the people and the people loved them in return. This was their territory and they were willing to defend it at all cost.

They achieved their goals by possessing the people, indoctrinating, manipulating, and dominating them. The people of Gadara desired the continued association with these spirits that manifested insanity of the worst kind as one of the side attractions of their manifestations. At least the way the elders reacted to Jesus' deliverance session corroborated this assertion. They were not interested in the miracles wrath, but were angered that Jesus allowed the demons to possess the herds of swine. Hence in spite of the man's deliverance and his being *'..clothed and in his right mind:...'* (Mk 5:15), the people were not impressed about what they saw but were repugnant or disgusted.

Even though the witnesses of the great miracle wrath at the deliverance of the man made attempts to share graphically the testimony of the great thing the Lord did, perhaps with the elders of the people but they were not moved. Their desire to send Jesus packing overshadowed the good Jesus did to the victim of territorial spirits. They rather thought Jesus to be an economic saboteur. to have allowed two thousand pigs drown in the sea!

Even though Jesus had ruffled some feathers in the realm of the spirit, the maintenance of the status quo was paramount in their heart. It was therefore not surprising that the people *'.. began to pray him to depart out of their coasts'*. (Mk 517). They were so filled with evil that like their forefathers (tribe of Gad) rejected the promise of crossing Jordan into the promise land, they also rejected Jesus and his miracles. They drove Jesus out of their coast and out of their lives. Hence they went out into perpetual darkness and obscurity, like Jonah 'from the presence of the Lord' (Jonah 1:3).

## *The case of Korah, Dothan and Abiram*

In the book of numbers we also see another biblical example of generation wasters in operation at the territorial level. In this account we see how through rebellion a generation of people were wasted at the move of God's judgment. The book of Num 16:2 tells us about Korah, Dothan, Abiram and:

> *'...two hundred and fifty princes of the assembly, famous in the congregation, men of renown.'*

These men challenged the priestly authority of Moses and Aaron. The Dakes Annotated Bible in page 174 second column in 'b' listed the 8 accusations against them viz.

1. You take too much upon you, and exercise more authority than you have the right (v3)

2. You think you are the only holy ones but all in the congregation are holy.

3. You lift yourselves up above the congregation of the Lord.

4. You have brought us out of Egypt, the real land of milk and honey, to kill us in the wilderness (v13)

5. You make yourself a prince over us.

6. You have not brought us into the promised land of milk and honey.

## DEALING WITH GENERATION WASTERS

7. You have not given us inheritance of fields and vineyards as you have promised.

8. You blind the eyes of the people to the fact that you keep none of your promises.

From the above summary one could see how in the book of Numbers, 'wasters' prepared the stage for the wasting of these people who ought to know better. When the spirits of destruction operate no amount of persuasion or good reasoning will prevail until their victim is ensnared in the trap of death set for him or her.

Hence the consequence of this rebellion was predictable as one thing God cannot stand is rebellion against authority at any level. In anger, the first thing Moses did was to make an appeal to God, standing on integrity cum holiness, to stand by him and his brother, Aaron and not follow popular opinion. (v15). He thereafter invited them to come before the Lord each man with his censer and incense for the Lord to choose his men. Foolishly they fell for this suicidal venture and:

*'..they took every man his censer, and put fire in them, and laid incense thereon, and stood in the of the tabernacle of the congregation with Moses and Aaron'.* (v18)

Immediately this was done the glory of the Lord appeared unto the entire congregation. A separation exercise was divinely conducted in order for God to bring two judgmental visitations to settle the matter at hand:

*'And the Lord spake unto Moses and unto Aaron, saying: Separate yourselves from this congregation,'* (v20-21).

The anger of God burnt so hurt that he was going to consume the congregation of the people, but the intercession of Moses and Aaron for God to deal with the actual sinners was answered. God therefore ordered separation from the camp of the wicked men. As soon as this was done, Moses asked circumspectly that God should do a new thing and allow the earth to swallow them up and judgment fell instantly. The Bible had this to say about the first judgment:

*'And it came to pass, as he had made an end of speaking all these words, that the ground clave asunder that was under him:*

*And the earth opened her mouth, and swallowed them up, and their houses, and all the men that appertained unto Korah, and all their goods.*

*They, and all that appertained to them, went down alive into the pit, and the earth closed upon them: and they perished from among the congregation.'* (v31-33)

The second type of judgment fell upon the two hundred and fifty men who had the audacity to carry their censers in deceit and wickedness before the Lord. While the earth opened to swallow up the families of Korah and his supporters, the heavens opened:

## DEALING WITH GENERATION WASTERS

*'And there came out a fire from the Lord, and consumed the two hundred and fifty men that offered incense.'* (v36).

These accounts sum up the manifestations of generation wasters, which in collaboration with territorial spirits and their demons mete death and destruction on their helpless victims.

The next chapter ushers us into how to deal with generation wasters. It opens our eyes to some depth of insights into their operation and root of the affliction. With these we are able to raise pertinent questions on the involvement of the family with the devil and the legal ground given to them to oppress. These are some of the factors that will help in applying the appropriate prayer strategy to silence the operation of evil forces over one' family.

# Chapter 4 - THE MANIFESTATIONS OF GENERATION WASTERS?

1. I come against the gathering of wasters with Holy Spirit consuming fire in Jesus name..

2. I resist your manifestations over my family and I in Jesus name.

3. I repent, renounce, and reject any legal reason that will enable you to operate in my family and I.

4. I command fire and brimstone to fall upon the priest and the altar of evil sacrifice raised against me.

5. I release fire and brimstone upon every covenant enforcer, limiting my lineage from going forward.

6. I command gates to be lifted up that the Lord's presence may come in.

7. All unknown agreement between my village, town or city with satanic gatekeepers are neutralized.

8. Every legal ground that my ancestors had given satanic powers to rule my lineage is overruled.

9. Let the light shine through darkness in Jesus name.

10. Every ploy of Satan is exposed in Jesus name.

# Chapter Five
# DEALING WITH GENERATION WASTERS

*"But upon mount Zion there shall be deliverance, there shall be holiness and the house of Jacob shall possess heir possession -" Obadiah 18*

## Introduction

In dealing with generation wasters, one must know the root of the affliction and have deep insight into their operations. There are processes involved while dealing with entities of darkness. Of course the issues of prayer, fasting and raising quality praise and worship that should usher one in the presence of God are quiet salient in the process of warfare.

The other areas of need include spiritual mapping, raising vital personal and general questions that may help to find answers to questions to be raised. One will need to trust the Lord for discernment and relevant grace in dealing with the case at hand.

However, for mere purpose of guidelines please find listed below some of the leading questions one may want to ask before proffering solutions to dealing with generation wasters. These questions may be modified, expanded to suit one's purpose as the spirit may direct.

i) What was the cause of the affliction

ii) How did it start?

iii) What was and is presently the family religion

iv) Were there commitments made to traditional gods?

v) If yes which gods?

vi) Were the commitments fulfilled?

vii) How was the god worshipped?

viii) What was the object of worship?

ix) How did the family get involved with the transactions?

x) Was it as a result of need or societal pressure?

xi) What were the names of the fathers involved in the contract?

xii) What were the terms of the covenant?

xiii) What were the tokens given?

xiv) What were the covenant responsibilities?

The knowledge of these will help in applying the appropriate prayer strategy to silence the influence of evil forces over the family. Of course one will need to lead the victims involved in repentance, renouncement, rejection and release (or deliverance) from the bondage.

## *The Wind Behind The Storm*

While one looks at the strategy of the Lord in dealing with the devil, it is observed that he handled such matters with divine wisdom. One obvious situation that attracts one's attention is in the gospel of Mark chapter 4 verses 37 to 41. In verse 37 we read that:

*"...there arose a great storm of wind, and the waves beat into the ship, so that it was now full"*

What was obvious to those in the ship was the storm, yet the Bible states the *'storm of wind..'*. It is salient to mention that it is not just a storm, but *'.. a great storm of wind'*. A storm of wind is one thing, while a great storm of wind is something else entirely. When you put these facts together, then you know what hope those in the ship had at that point in time. Indeed, without the Lord Jesus Christ it was a hopeless situation.

However, while the storm raged, the Lord and the master of creation slept in the hinder part of the ship. This was not a Jonah caught by the power of sleep, but the one that is the full manifestation of peace. He could sleep because all things in heaven and earth were subject to him. They were all the creation of his hand. Yet this unusual peace in the midst of crisis infuriated the disciples who lacked the knowledge of who Jesus was and still is. So in their fear and frustration they went to:

> ***"..awake him, and say unto him, Master, carest thou not that we perish?"*** *(v38).*

They were more concerned about themselves than about Jesus. In response to their cry the Prince of Peace arose in the midst of this terrible situation and all the enemies began to scatter. Because He is beautiful for every situation, He knew what to do. Notice that in verse 39 the Bible declares that: ***"..he arose, and rebuked the wind, and said unto the sea Peace be still…."***.

Why did he not rebuke the storm? Why the wind? This is because there is a power behind the storm, which in effect means there are powers behind every spiritual problem. This example is to open our eyes to the fact that most of the time we address the symptoms rather than the root of the problem. The Lord of all knowledge went straight to the root and rebuked it and said to the sea peace be still. At his dealing with the roots the Bible informs us that ***"….the wind ceased, and there was a great calm."***

Do you notice he did not even mention the storm? That is the problem many of us are facing. A woman is barren and all we begin to bind is barrenness instead of identifying the root cause. For example, there is the story of a woman who traded her fruitfulness for wealth, and in pretence went from place to place hoping to receive her breakthrough. She never owned up, neither did she repent in spite of the obvious concern of the church and her husband who were 'punished' through unending vigils and fasting.

However we thank God for the man of God whom God opened his eyes, perhaps to show mercy to the people involved in her case. He challenged the woman about the satanic contract with her fertility and insisted on her repentance and renouncement. She tearfully confessed her wicked contract, repented, and renounced it. The man of God rebuked the power behind the barrenness, her breakthrough came instantly, and she became a mother thereafter. This confirms that every problem has its symptoms as well as root cause. There is always a root to a problem.

## *Hear His Counsel*

Since there is a wind behind the storm we face in life, it is important to rely on the counsel of the lord in times like this and always. The counsel of the Lord is crucial in order to overcome in spiritual warfare. The same is required, in order to also survive this present evil world. Somehow men do not hear, not just because they wish it to be so but it is because they are under some inexplicable influences beyond their control. It is obvious to all that the line they tow is fraught with danger, but they obstinately forge ahead in spite of all odds. Yet they seem to forget that: *"Whatever you sow, you shall reap..."*

It is a sign of the fact that the servant is blind and the messenger deaf as revealed in Isaiah Chapter 42. So how can the servant perform and the messenger deliver the message? It will take divine intervention to bring solutions to the people because they themselves need help. It is obvious that the blindness and deafness of the messenger are spiritual. The Bible confirms in verse 20 that:

> *'Seeing many things, but thou observest not; opening the ears, but he heareth not.'*

Yet the work must go on in spite of this and for his

> *"... righteousness' sake; he will magnify the law, and make it honourable."* (v21)

The law is the word of God. This is the reason that in some cases in spite of us the word of God goes ahead to perform what it is sent forth to do. It is his promise to *"..magnify the law, and make it honourable"*, that is being fulfilled. The word is made honorable when the blind sees, the deaf hears, the barren gets pregnant, the sick healed and the poor gets rich. Where this is to the contrary, it means we have subjected ourselves willingly to open robbery and allowed our resources and ourselves to be wasted by the powers of darkness.

## DEALING WITH GENERATION WASTERS

Furthermore, it means we have allowed them to take the initiative, and are subjected very willingly to their whims and caprices. Yet the word of the Lord has gone forth to open the prison door and usher us out into the land with milk and honey. Liberty has been given to us on platter of gold, yet we remain lukewarm expecting another miracle to move us forward, when God who had done the work had said to us: ***"Ye have compassed this mountain long enough: turn you northward"*** (Deut. 2:3).

In spite of this, some are still living in the valley of despair and hoping that one day, they will be free. The contract guaranteeing their freedom had been signed, sealed, and delivered. Yet they do not know this, because they are blind and deaf. The reality in some cases is that some enjoy hanging around their mountain (problems), because of the sympathy they receive from people. God is saying turn to me and I will help you. Turning northward is turning towards the city of God and his throne is in: ***"...mount Zion, on the sides of the north, the city of the great king."*** (Ps. 48:2).

In mount Zion, God is beautiful for every situation, no matter what. All one needs is just to trust him because he never disappoints. Hence, one needs to rise up and take the battle to the enemy's doorsteps.

## Strategic Warfare Against Generation Wasters

In dealing with the generation wasters one requires some level of insight into the word of God for effective spiritual warfare. This insight will enable one to develop effective strategies to handle them. In this respect the book of Nahum Chapter 2 verse 1 proffers solution.

> *'He that dasheth in pieces is come up before thy face: keep the munition, watch the way, make thy loins strong, fortify thy power mightily.'*

## Strategies/Weapons

The basic strategies identified above are also weapons one should apply when dealing with them. The knowledge of these will assist the intercessor to hit at the foundation of generation wasters in a person's life. The verse introduces one to four strategies that can be used to deal with *'He that dasheth in pieces..'*, which is better known as generation waster. These four biblical strategies are listed below:

1. Keep the munition,

2. Watch the way,

3. Make thy loins strong,

4. Fortify thy power mightily.

## *i) Keep The Munition*

In order to successfully prosecute a war, it is only wise to have enough stock of weapons and ammunition for battle. This thought however, presupposes that one has enough men to effectively handle them. Hence, in the book of Isaiah, we are informed about the portion of the upright man if he dares to confront the enemy in battle.

The first thing he must do is to appear before the Lord whose throne is in Zion. He must be a man of holiness to receive answer to his prayer. This is basically the reason we find the statement made in the book Isaiah 33 verse 14:

> *'The sinners in Zion are afraid: fearfulness hath surprised the hypocrites...'*

Why? This is simply because there must be holiness upon the mount of Zion. Apart from being a place of holiness, Mount Zion is a place of deliverance and possessing of our possessions (Oba 18). The same is where the throne of God '...whose fire is in Zion..' (Is 31:9) is situated. No wonder the question '...who among us shall dwell with the devouring fire?...' (Is. 33:14).

The next verse gives us a list of requirements that one can summarize as pertaining to the one who is righteous or upright. This is the one who can '..dwell with everlasting burnings.' Beyond this, the book intimates us with other weapons available to the man apart from holiness and fire that he should generate from the Lord's presence. The 16$^{th}$ verse tells us that

*'He shall dwell on high: his place of defence shall be the munitions of rocks…'*

Our God is a man of war. He is a land (Army), sea (Navy), and sky (Air Force) general. We saw how he deployed stones or rocks in dealing with the enemy in the book of Joshua. He was the first Air Force General to carry out the aerial bombardment of his enemies.

Even though the enemy suffered heavy casualties in the hand of God's land army, but time was running out as nighttime was fast approaching. Joshua issued a decree for the sun and moon to stand still, in order for the army to have light to fight yet there was still much battle to be fought.

However, the Bible tells us how God strategically came to their rescue and concluded the battle in Israel's favor in Joshua Chapter 10 verse 11:

*"And it came to pass, as they fled from before Israel and were in the going down to Beth-horon, that the Lord cast down great stones from heaven upon them unto Azekah, and they died:."*

Our God is the greatest war strategist, who knows what to do in every situation. At the end of the day, the aerial bombardment of the enemy forces accounted for more death than the land army could have done as we read in the same verse that there:

*'...were more which died with hailstones than they whom the children of Israel slew with the sword.'*

What a great God we serve!

In addition to the munition of the rocks, one should also apply the precious cornerstone of our salvation in warfare. This stone is *"..in Zion for a foundation a stone, a tried stone, a precious corner stone, a sure foundation..."* (Is. 28:16).

As you pray you must stand on this verse as your foundation for the battle. The stone is both a foundation (weapon of defense) and stone of assault (weapon of offence). Command the stone to sink into the forehead of the enemy (Goliath) and break its feet into pieces like the image of Daniel 2:34.

Finally, one can also use other weapons mentioned in the Bible such as the hammer and sword of God's word; the name and blood of Jesus, the east wind, and the fire of the Holy Spirit etc. These weapons can be effectively utilized in worded prayers, copiously quoting relevant portions of the Bible. One must be well grounded in the word of God to effectively fight at this level of warfare.

## *ii) Watch The Way*

This is specifically requesting a need to monitor happenings around you through prayers. An intercessor must set a watch, in order to declare what he sees especially when prayer project is set on a particular problem (Isaiah 21:6). Dealing with powers of darkness requires divine intervention; hence one must hear clearly from God the direction to take. Divine instructions help one to walk on the path of truth when decision just must be taken. There is a need to be careful in every action taken in order not to fall into the hands of the devil, by acting in the flesh. This is why it is very important to *'Watch and pray, that ye enter not into temptation...'* (Mt 26:41)

It is important to know the source and legal reason for its existence, having recognized the existence of the problem. This statement holds true and indeed pays off if one is *'... sober, and watch unto prayer'* (I Pet 4:7). When one is also able to apply godly wisdom in what he sees the solution will come quicker than expected. That revelation is a key issue in spiritual warfare cannot be over emphasized. When dealing with generation wasters it becomes a need that is much more salient. This truth will enable the intercessor to have specific instructions from God's throne on what to do.

Applying this in one's life is also crucial. It is easier to preempt the enemy than resisting after he has taken dominion. There is a grave danger in not watching in prayer. In fact, the Bible tells us *'But watch thou in all things..'* (2 Tim 4:5). While still on this and its implication the story of John the Baptist readily comes to mind. The wasters planned his execution and he knew not. The enemy shot the arrows of doubt at him for starters. He sent men to ask Jesus after hearing the miracles he was performing: *'Art thou he that should come, or do we look for another?'* (Mt 11:3).

This was an ancestral problem emanating from his father to him. His father Zecharias doubted the angel's message, that Elizabeth his wife would conceive and bear a child. (Lk 1:11-18).

John doubted the same Jesus whom he declared *'...I saw the Spirit descending from heaven like a dove, and it abode upon him.'* (Jn 1:32).

Herod threw him into prison, because he confronted him on his relationship with Herodias his brother Philip's wife. This was the loophole Satan used against him and the spirit of confusion took over from that point. The Lord Jesus in answer to his question showed his disappointment by saying:

> *'Go and shew John again those things which ye do hear and see:..'* (v4).

Please notice the words *'Go and shew John again..'*. That to me connotes nothing but the fact that John had heard about these things before. Yet the ancestral doubt operating in his family affected him from believing the truth. The spirit got to him, because he failed to watch the way effectively. If only he had kept the watch as advised by the Lord Jesus, perhaps this ought not to have happened.

## iii) Make Thy Loins Strong

Making your loins strong speaks of the ability to tarry long in prayers. This basically is a strategic advice to be prepared and be ready to confront the powers of darkness. When you are strong in the Lord and in the power of his might nothing can overwhelm you.

There is a need to be ready for both expected and unexpected battles. You must make strength available in spiritual warfare by taking a serious decision in this regard.

> *'Stand therefore, having your loins girt about with truth, and having on the breastplate of righteousness;'* - (Eph 6:14)

The above is the picture of a Roman soldier in military regalia and clad in various kinds of armor. Every part of the armor must be put in place and this cannot be done in a hurry. Somebody must partner with you to put it on, which also suggest two in agreement in prayer.

However, the only part of the soldier's body exposed was his back, since he was not expected to turn his back to his enemy in battle. He must confront every enemy face to face. Anyone that died with stab wound on his back brought shame to his family, because it meant he was running away from battle when the enemy stabbed him. Therefore he must fight back to back without breaking ranks with another partner soldier in his platoon. This form of fighting guaranteed protection of his and his partner's back in battle. This is one of the reasons the Church of God emphasizes the need for prayer partner.

It must of a necessity be the whole armor or else one is courting disaster. When the pieces of armor are in place, they ensure that no part of the soldier's body is exposed. He must be covered from head to toes, because any uncovered frontal part of his body could spell disaster, as the enemy would take advantage of this chink in the armor to do damage.

It is the whole armor that can guarantee protection and help in the time of battle. Any thing short of this is taking a long journey into failure. Why must one put on the whole armor of God? It is *'..so that ye may be able to stand against the wiles of the devil. ...'* (Eph. 6:11).

To successfully achieve the above, the person involved in battle must *'..be strong in the Lord, and in the power of his might. ....'* His source of strength must only be from the Lord. He must not compromise this requirement in any way or else he may be preparing himself for disaster. The tricks of the devil are numerous, one of it is to get you in a hurry. The way to douse it is to put on all manner of prayers. This is because the entities we are wrestling against are not:

*'...flesh and blood, but against principalities, against powers, against the rulers of the darkness of this world, against spiritual wickedness in high places.'* (Eph. 6:12)

When the need to do battle is identified, it is important to run into the presence of the Lord, to seek His face and draw more strength from Him. To succeed in battle, one must wait patiently on God until He defines the battle strategies and gives one the go ahead. He determines the waiting period required. No matter the time specified, it is better to wait, because one does not know how the battle may turn out. Only God knows, so it is better to consult Him. While in His presence, one will receive grace and divine enablement and he will honor one by giving one the blue print for battle. This is what it means to make your loins strong.

## *iv) Fortify Your Power Mightily*

This simply encourages one to reinforce his power base. When your power is made stronger and the enemy knows this, he will seriously avoid you till he finds an auspicious moment of weakness to strike. The Bible in Isaiah 40:31 gives an insight into this fortification:

> *'But they that wait upon the Lord shall renew their strength;.'*

When a man fasts he renews lost energy in battle. The renewed strength actually conveys the meaning of fortified or increased strength. The strength is on the increase and is empowered to do exploits in God. At that point in time whatsoever you bind on earth is bound in heaven. You are able to engage in serious spiritual warfare without any fear of danger. The power to be victorious has been received in the place of fasting and prayers. Hence, beyond just renewal of strength,

> *".... they shall mount up with wings as eagles; they shall run, and not be weary; and they shall walk and not faint.* (Is. 40:31).

The above verse describes three categories of Christians: those that operate at the level of eagle saints (Elisha Company); they that run and do not go weary (Elijah Company) and those that walk and not faint (Samson Company). Please find these briefly enumerated below.

### a) *The Elisha Company*

The first category best fit Elisha, who by the grace of God performed thirty-two major miracles in his ministry, and these are those that mount up with wings as eagles. They operate at a higher frequency of power in the heavenlies.

In his time, Elisha was just too much for his generation. Here was a man that a whole battalion was sent to arrest because he was instrumental to knowing what was happening in the king's palace (II kings 6). Hence he made nonsense of their war plans or strategies to the utter embarrassment of the King and his military commanders, who thought somebody on their side must have been leaking war secrets to the king of Israel.

When it was discovered that the person behind their problem was Elisha, he sent a whole battalion to arrest one man because he knew his antecedents as a dangerous man - one who knew what was going in the King's bedroom. When the soldiers got there and he saw them, he saw more soldiers in the spirit than those in the physical. All he simply did was to pray that the Lord should hit 6,000 soldiers with blindness.

Instantly, 6000 pairs of eyes got blinded just like that! Gehazi, his servant, who was intimidated by the number of soldiers, was prayed for and God opened his to see the angelic support God sent to protect them. Such was the power of this man that even in his death his bones raised another dead man back to life

*'.... and when the (dead) man was let down, and touched the bones of Elisha, he revived, and stood up on his feet.'* (II Kings 13:21b)

I remember the story of a sister who was challenged by Sango (god of Thunder) worshippers for daring to sell her wares when orders have gone out that no shops should open. She told the leaders of the team in plain term that she had consulted with her father and she had received confirmation to come out and sell. She went further to tell them that her father owned the "*.... earth and its fullness thereof...*"

Her audacity infuriated the men and they told her that her father would weep with her by the time they finished dealing with her. Meanwhile, they did not know that she was referring to the Almighty God as her father. She affirmed categorically that they could do her nothing because:

## DEALING WITH GENERATION WASTERS

*"No weapon that is formed against her shall prosper.."* (Isaiah 54:17)

In the heat of the trading of words, the leader of the Sango team said to her:

**"For all you have said in your arrogance, you will die within seven days".**

She promptly replied by telling him I *'...will not die but live to declare the glory of the Lord in the land of the living.'*

Having said that she concluded with the clincher "**If my father is the living God that dwells in the heavenly places, all of you will not last three days on earth. But if he is not then I will die."**

On that note they parted in anger unable to touch her. However the words of God caught up with them within three days specified by the woman. Judgment day came, God confirmed the words of her daughter, and there was commotion in the community. She lived but her enemies perished. That is the fruit of being an eagle saint in the place of prayer.

### ii) The Elijah Company

The second category, which is *'... they shall run, and not be weary;'* is the picture of Elijah who by the grace of God performed sixteen major miracles in his ministry. He was that man that the Bible tells us the I Kings 18:46 that:

> *'.. the hand of the Lord was upon Elijah; and he girded up his loins, and ran before Ahab to the entrance of Jezreel'*

The presence of the Lord was so overwhelming that this man under the anointing of the Holy Spirit out ran a man who was riding in his chariot.

What inspired this happening? There was no rain for three years because Elijah decided so through the help of God in order to deal with Ahab and Israel. He challenged the Baal worshippers to call on their god to answer by fire by consuming the sacrifice placed on the altar. Baal failed its people after hours of unending but fruitless cries, but the God of Elijah answered by fire and consumed the sacrifice. As a result all the priest of Baal were slaughtered that day. Having dealt with the priests of Baal, he told:

> *'...Ahab, Get thee up, eat and drink; for there is a sound of abundance of rain.'* (I kings 18:41).

Between the two of them, it was obvious who would be an instrument of the expected miracle. Ahab went up to the mountain to eat, while Elijah went up to pray. While Ahab was busy attending to the flesh, the one that runs and do not weary was monitoring the happenings in the heavens until his servant saw *'...a little cloud out of the sea, like a man's hand...'*(v44). It is important to mention the resilience of the man who sent his servant to *'...Go again seven times...'* to monitor what the heavens would release.

As soon as he got clear understanding of God's move, he told Ahab

> *'...Prepare thy chariot, and get thee down, that the rain stop thee not.'* (v44).

The man of God did not consider himself; neither did Ahab who was all flesh bothered to ask how Elijah was to get home before the heavens poured its content. We thank God that Ahab did not invite Elijah to join him in his chariot, and also that Elijah did not ask to join him. This would have robbed him of the miracle God was about to do. The bible tells us:

> *'...And Ahab rode, and went to Jezreel. And the hand of the Lord was on Elijah; and he girded up his loins, and ran before Ahab to the entrance of Jezreel'* (v45-46).

The presence of the Lord was so overwhelming that this man under the anointing of the Holy Spirit out ran a man who was riding in his chariot. Alleluia!

### *iii) The Samson Company*
The third category is a clear manifestation of all that Samson represents, *'..and they shall walk and not faint.'* The man Samson had very great potentials but for the flesh – his character flaws limited him. He was so-to-speak like a chicken saint permanently fixed to the ground. Unlike the eagle saints this man could not fly, but only walk. His divine ability strengthened him a great deal *'...to walk and not faint.'*

Samson was such a spoilt child that he was always after the things God did not approve of. He was a man raised in the period of lawlessness and faithlessness and was largely influenced by the conducts of his age. Even though his parents showed clear evidence of faith and righteousness, yet Samson was a product of his terrible time. His parent's faithfulness and commitment to God did not stop him from being caught by the bug eating men alive in his time. The refrain in those days as accounted by the writer of the book of Judges was:

***'In those days there was no king in Israel, but every man did that which was right in his own eyes.'*** (Judg. 17:6)

One can arguably say that his first encounter with a Philistine woman of Timnath was of the Lord because God:

***'... sought an occasion against the Philistines: for at that time the Philistines had dominion over Israel.'*** (Judg 14:4).

While this encounter was supposed to be an exception, Samson took it to be the rule. This first encounter with a woman led him from one woman to another until he was destroyed in the laps of Delilah.

Even though the spirit of the Lord was very strong upon him, there was no clear evidence of his submission to the things of the spirit in working righteousness. His weakness for pagan women was legendary. He was almost captured in Gaza when he went to visit a prostitute (Judg. 16:1-3). In spite of his great potentials, sin and disobedience limited him. He was mighty in strength, yet weak in morals and resisting temptation.

What revealed itself clearly in his short life was the spirit of vengeance. Since he never gave himself much to the word of God he probably did not imbibe the fact that Deuteronomy 32 verse 35 states the mind of God that *'Vengeance is mine'* Yet we saw him taking vengeance against those who used devious means to get information about his riddles in Judges Chapter 14:12-20.

We see the same vengeful spirit in Judges 15:6-7 when his father-in-law gave away his wife to another man. In spite of his great strength, he was a fool - a clear evidence of being a man limited by the flesh. There was no evidence of strategic planning in the execution of his one-man war. He was all strength but no tact and this is simply because *'Wisdom is too high for a fool....'* (Prov. 24:7). His attack on this occasion caused him the loss of his wife as: *'...the Philistines came up, and burnt her and her father with fire.'* (Judg. 15:6).

The same devious means his wife used to break the riddles was what Delilah used. He was a man weak in resolution in the presence of a persistent woman. He could not draw the line between deception and truth. The tears of a 'fair weather' woman made a man's strength to crumble. He played into her hands, and gave out the secret of his strength and cut short God's purpose for his life. The investment of God in him to save the nation was aborted in the house of a pagan woman. He never did fly; he was kept at the level of walking until the race ended for him abruptly.

It is pertinent at this point to note, however that the Bible records an enviable victory at his death over his enemy to the point that:

*'..the dead which he slew at his death were more than they which he slew in his life.'* (Judg. 16:30).

It may interest one to ask how many people did he kill? In verse 27 we read the following:

*'..and there were upon the roof about three thousand men and women, that beheld Samson made sport.'*

If you take time to look into the scriptures, and do a comparative analysis of this man with David the man after God's heart you will discover that they were not up to those David killed in one battle. David was always killing his 10,000 while Saul's own was 1,000. Samson hence never rose to the potentials God desired for him because:

*'…by means of a whorish woman a man is brought to a piece of bread:..'* (Prov. 6:26)

*'For her house inclineth unto death, and her paths unto the dead. None that go unto her return again, neither take they hold of the paths of life.'* (Prov. 2:18-19)

# Chapter 5: **MANIFESTATIONS OF GENERATION WASTERS**

1. I decree that my life attract blessing, success, victory and breakthroughs today in Jesus name.

2. Let my light so shine that my enemies will be the ones to advertise my blessings in Jesus name.

3. Just as the fish that swallowed Jonah vomited him, let all the troubles of life that had swallowed me up vomit me.

4. O Lord! In your mercy hiss for me and gather me for blessings in Jesus name.

5. O Lord sow me among the people, and let me grow so that I may remember you in far countries.

6. O Lord make me a terror to the enemy in the name of Jesus.

7. Spirit of the living God let all my enemies weep, as I climb the ladder of success they thought impossible.

8. O Lord! I paralyze every plan of Satan to recycle suffering for me.

9. In Jesus name I shall not die before my glory comes.

10. O Lord! Smite every satanic and oppressive horse of my life with astonishment by giving me victory over it.

# Chapter Six
# THE GENERATION OF WICKEDNESS?

*'....I created the waster to destroy.' - Isaiah 54:16*

## *Introduction*

One of the things this evil being cannot compromise is their art of destruction. They are raised to kill, to steal, and to destroy. They specialize in afflicting and wasting the lives of generations of people. There is no way of escape except one is under the covering of the blood of Jesus and has renounced all legal hold that the enemy can refer to. As mentioned in the earlier chapter of this book, legal holds are the covenants or transactions the forefathers had entered into with the forces of darkness. As long as these covenants stand there can be no peace for that family and its generation born or yet to be born.

Several generations down the line are under the clutches of entities of darkness against their will. This is due to their ignorance in entering into covenant with them. The enemy does not joke with the terms of the covenant and where there is a default the covenant enforcers move in viciously against their victim. This is why it is important to reject and renounce covenants or evil transactions entered into by one or on one's behalf.

Through satanic covenants generation wasters have put the generations born and unborn into perpetual bondage, because of the carelessness of their fathers. No matter where they run, their case files will precede them there and the covenant enforcers will deal worse with them. We have seen the generation wasters in operation in various parts of the bible as highlighted in the previous chapter. Their operations have always been known to be very ruthless and without mercy. In short, their specific assignment is to steal, kill, and destroy.

A brief look into Herod dynasty may help us to see how these powers raised wickedness to a higher pedestal and preyed on the souls of innocent men.

# *The Blood-filled Reigns of Herod Dynasties*

The bible reveals to us several leaders named Herod and how their reigns of terror procured for their people sorrow, tears and bloodshed. The Nelson's

## DEALING WITH GENERATION WASTERS

New Illustrated Bible Dictionary in page 559 gives us an insight into the history or the foundation of the descendants of Herod. The title Herod is:

> '...the name of several Roman rulers in the Palestine region during Jesus' earthly ministry and the periods shortly before His birth and after His resurrection.
>
> The Herodian dynasty made its way into Palestine through Antipater, an Idumean by descent. The Idumeans were of Edomite stock as descendants of Esau. Antipater was installed as procurator of Rome, in 47 B.C. He appointed his sons into ruling positions. One of these was "Herod the Great," who was appointed governor of Judae'

Without any doubt, if we draw our conclusions from the information gathered from the bible, the Edomite root of the Herods clearly explains the reason for the wickedness perpetrated by this ruling clan. The Edomites were the descendants of Esau and we are aware of how this man, careless for spiritual things lost his birthright and wanted to kill his sup-planter brother, Jacob.

It is also revealed to us in Ps 137 verse 7 how Edom was involved in the massive destruction of Jerusalem and the people. These satanic traits were largely influenced by the entities of darkness controlling their ancestral fathers. These spirits dominated almost all the lineage in varying degrees of wickedness with the exception of Herod Philip.

## i) Herod the Great

The history of the founding fathers has revealed the forces controlling this ancestral line. However, the flow of the blood of wickedness running in the veins of Herod family was taken to greater heights through Herod the Great whose middle name could simply be called wickedness. He was uniquely positioned as wickedness personified - a terrain in which a willing contender for this trophy was difficult to find. The Nelson's New Illustrated Bible Dictionary in page 559 tells us that:

> 'The title Herod the Great refers not so much to Herod's greatness as to the fact that he was the eldest son of Antipater. Nevertheless, Herod did show some unusual abilities. He was a ruthless fighter, a cunning negotiator, and a subtle diplomat. The Romans appreciated the way he subdued opposition and maintained order among the Jewish people.'

The testimony to his ruthlessness, cunning approach to matters, and vicious strategy was how he tricked the wise men to go and get him information on the new born baby so that he could come and worship him. However, the wise men being warned of God never returned to him.

*'Then Herod when he saw that he was mocked of the wise men, was exceeding wroth, and sent forth, and slew all the children that were in Bethlehem, and in all the coasts thereof, from two years old and under, according to the time*

*which he had diligently inquired of the wise men.'* (Mt 2:16)

That he ordered the slaughter of all these innocent male infants whom he thought one of them (Jesus) could possibly be considered legal heir to the throne was unimaginable. His acts of morbid callousness and lack of human feelings were legendary! He did it anyhow and ensured that children within the age bracket specified were killed. Can you imagine the number of children generation wasters made this wicked man kill? Almost every home was affected and: the bible prophesied through Jeremiah this sordid event thus:

*'In Rama was there a voice heard, lamentation, and weeping, and great mourning, Rachel weeping for her children, and would not be comforted, because they are not'* (Mt 2:18).

These spirits were not done with him yet, they moved him to murder his wife Mariamme and crowned his wickedness with the silencing of his two sons Alexander and Aristobulus. These two apparently knew that he murdered their mother and foolishly challenged him. They paid dearly with their lives.

## ii) Herod Archelaus

The second Herod, inherited his father's vices without his abilities and was responsible for much bloodshed in Judae and Samaria. This man brutally crushed the revolts led by the zealots. Herods Antipas and Philip did not approve his methods and they complained to

Rome and followed it up with a Jewish delegation that succeeded in ensuring his being stripped of power and banished to Rome. The evil had however been done.

The only bible reference to him is seen in Mt 2:22 where Joseph was afraid to go to Judae when he heard that Archelaus reigned in there after his father's death. God however warned Joseph in a dream to go to the regions of Galilee.

### iii) Herod Philip the Tetrarch

This was one of the best of the ruling Herods and was about the only one that did not fall prey to the domination of generation wasters. He was one of those that reported Herod Archelaus' wicked reign to Rome, which caused his being stripped of power and banished to Rome.

We saw him introduced in Lk 3:1 as the '...tetrarch of Ituraea and of the region of Trachonitis.' It was during his time that '...the word of God came unto John the son of Zacharias in the wilderness.' (v2). Coupled with the spiritual revolution in his time, he was able to carry out laudable building projects, which included the city of Caesarea, Philippi, as well as rebuilding Bethsaida into a Greek city and renamed it Julias in honor of Augustus Caesar's daughter, Julia.

### iv) Herod Antipas

This was the ruling Herod during Jesus' life and ministry. The spirit of wickedness got hold of him when he became infatuated with Herodias, the wife

## DEALING WITH GENERATION WASTERS

of his half-brother, Philip I. Even though married, both of them eloped to enjoy the pleasure of sin for a season. To his embarrassment, John the Baptist openly condemned this sinful affair and he had him arrested and imprisoned as a result.

However, events later revealed that Herodias was not just pleased with just mere imprisonment. She desired worse punitive measure and therefore waited for the right time. The opportunity to strike, later presented itself at a royal birthday party Antipas held. Herod granted Salome the daughter of Herod Philip and Herodias a wish and

*'...she being before instructed of her mother, said, Give me here John Baptist's head in a charger'.* (Mt 14:8).

Notice the words,

*'she being before instructed of her mother'*

These words made it clear that it was Herodias unforgiving spirit that got John Killed. Herod Antipas was caught in the web of foolish vow that he could not possibly have extricated himself. Therefore, being under oath and was not willing to lose face before his numerous guests and associates ordered the execution of John. Generation wasters again claimed another victim through murderous hatred.

## v) Herod Agrippa I

Herod Agrippa I took over from Antipas who as a follow up to John's death began to experience political turmoil in his domain. This led to his political downfall and eventual banishment to an obscure part of France. While growing up in the imperial court, as a young man, he developed an undisciplined attitude and extravagant life-style. He opposed the early church by killing James and arrested Peter in order to kill him also, because he saw that it pleased the Jews Acts (12:1-3). But thank God the whole Church prayed and Peter was delivered from the clutches of the destroyer because *'...the snare is broken, and we are escaped'* (PS 124:7).

## vi) Herod Agrippa II

This man who was considered too young to assume the throne of his father ushered the end of the Herodian dynasty. He was the one that listened to the defense of Paul in Acts 25:22-26, and the Apostle appealed to Rome because Agrippa II had no power to set him free.

# *The Martyrs*

In order to further understand the operation and manifestation of this evil spirits let us briefly advance our study to cover the Christian Martyrs. Many of them were killed because of their faith in Christ Jesus. The book of Hebrews in Chapter 11 gives us a panoramic view of some of the things done to them:

*'....and others were tortured, not accepting deliverance; that they might obtain a better resurrection.*

*And others had trial of cruel mockings and scourgings, yea, moreover of bonds and imprisonment:*

*They were stoned, they were sawn asunder, were tempted, were slain with the sword: they wandered about in sheepskins and goatskins; being destitute, afflicted, tormented;*

*(of whom the world was not worthy:) they wandered in deserts, and in mountains, and in dens and caves of the earth.'* (Heb 11:35-38)

From this biblical perspective, one can see how so far back the devil had gone in his war *'..to steal, and to kill and to destroy:....'* (Jn 10:10). His business of killing those who stand on the ground of truth had been on for ages and he is never tired but waxing strong in evil. It is only God that can help us to stop him in our individual life. This can only be made possible if we can believe and trust him enough to do so.

I wish to refer, at this point, to the opening comment of John Foxe in Chapter one of his book Foxe's Book of Martyrs titled **'History of Christian Matyrs To The First General Persecutions Under Nero'**. This will lay for the reader a good foundation and help him to have a better picture on this subject.

'Christ our Savior, in the Gospel of St. Matthew, hearing the confession of Simon Peter, who, first of all other, openly acknowledged Him to be the Son of God and perceiving the secret hand of His Father therein, called him (alluding to his name) a rock, upon which rock He would build His Church so strong that the gates of hell should not prevail against it. In which words three things are to be noted: First, that Christ will have a Church in this world. Secondly, that the same Church should mightily be impugned, not only by the world, but also by the uttermost strength and powers of all hell. And, thirdly, that the same Church, notwithstanding the uttermost of the devil and all his malice, should continue.

Which prophecy of Christ we see wonderfully to be verified, insomuch that the whole course of the Church to this day may seem nothing else but a verifying of the said prophecy. First, that Christ hath set up a Church, needeth no declaration. Secondly, what force of princes, kings, monarchs, governors, and rulers of this world, with their subjects, publicly and privately, with all their strength and cunning, have bent themselves against this Church! And, thirdly, how the said Church, all this notwithstanding, hath yet endured and holden its own! '

That the devil had declared a war against the church is an understatement. On every area of ground the church wishes to possess there is a willing opposition. Such oppositions that obviously take away people's lives just for professing Christ. Several religious crises have their roots in these deadly oppositions of hell. An unending lists of men who stood gallantly in death, and humbled the powers of hell abound. Briefly discussed below are just a few of them.

## I. Stephen

Stephen, one of the Deacons chosen to handle the work, was killed because of his faithfulness to the preaching of the Gospel to the betrayers and murderers of Christ. They were so enraged that they cast him out of the city and stoned him to death. It is interesting to note that not less than two thousand Christians, with Nicanor one of the seven deacons, suffered martyrdom during the persecution that arose about Stephen.

## II. James the Great

According to Acts of the Apostles, the next martyr in line was James the son of Zebedee. Just ten years after the death of Stephen, the second martyrdom took place. Herod Agrippa raised a sharp persecution against the Christians because he wanted to please the Jews. An eminent primitive writer, Clemens Alexandrinus, confirmed that James extraordinary courage at the point of death brought his accuser to repent of his conduct, confess Jesus as Lord and fell down at his feet to request his pardon. Both of them were beheaded at the same time. At about the same time, two other Christians were martyred: these were Timon at Philippi, and Parmenas at Macedonia in AD 44.'

## III. Philip
He was a native of Bethsaida, in Galilee and was first called by the name of "disciple". He worked in God's vineyard in Upper Asia. His labour for Christ was cut short by his arrest, scourging, imprisonment, and crucifixion at Heliopolis, in Phrygia in A. D. 54.

## IV. Matthew
A native of Nazareth, a tax collector and an Apostle of Jesus who wrote one of the gospels. His gospel was however written in Hebrew and later translated into Greek by James the Less. He laboured in Parthia, and Ethiopia, where he was slain in the city of Nadabah in AD 60.

## V. James the Less
He was the author of the Epistle of James and the overseer of the churches of Jerusalem. He was beaten, stoned and finally clubbed to death with a fuller's club by the Jews at the age of ninety-four.

## VI. Matthias
He was elected to fill the place of Judas. He was stoned and then beheaded at Jerusalem.

## VII. Andrew
The one that *'..first findeth his brother Simon (Peter)...'* (Jn 1:41). He labored in many Asiatic nations but terminated the race at Edessa where he was crucified on a cross, the two ends of which were fixed

transversely in the ground. This is the reason for the derivation of the term, St. Andrew's cross.

## VIII. Mark
He was a Jew of the tribe of Levi. A convert of Peter, whom he served and under whose inspection he wrote his Gospel in the Greek language. He was dragged through the streets of Alexandria untill he was torn to pieces, during the great solemnity of Serapis their idol.

## IX. Peter
He was an apostle of Jesus and brother of Andrew who considered himself unworthy to die after the same form and manner as the Lord Jesus did. He therefore requested to be crucified in inverted position.

## X. Paul
Apostle Paul, who was first called Saul, labored and suffered a great deal while promoting the Gospel of Christ, especially in places where it had not been preached. He was not spared in this first persecution under Nero. It was on record that Nero sent two of his esquires (Ferega and Parthemius) to witness his execution. This special delegation met him instructing the people, and asked him to pray for them, that they might believe. He told them that shortly after they should believe and be baptized at His sepulcher. Thereafter, the soldiers came and led him out of the city to the place of execution, where he, after praying gave his neck to the sword.

## XI. Jude
Brother Jude, who was commonly called Thaddeus, was the brother of James. He was crucified at Edessa in AD 72.

## XII. Bartholomew
Even though he preached in several countries, he did a more remarkable work in India, where he translated the Gospel of Matthew into the language of India, and propagated it there. Some impatient idolaters later arrested him; beat him thoroughly and then had him crucified.

## XIII. Thomas
He was called Didymus, and known generally as 'unbelieving Thomas'. He preached the Gospel in Parthia and India and was arrested by enraged pagan priests and martyred by being thrust through with a spear.

## XIV. Luke
The writer of the Gospel of Luke, a fellow traveler in the work with Paul the Apostle was arrested and supposed to have been hanged on an olive tree, by the idolatrous priests of Greece.

## XV. Simon
He was surnamed Zelotes, and he preached the Gospel in Mauritania in Africa, and Britain where he was crucified in AD 74.

## XVI. John

John the "beloved" was brother to James the Great. He founded the churches of Smyrna, Pergamos, Sardis, Philadelphia, Laodicea, and Thyatira. There was an order from Rome that he should be sent there. He was therefore taken from Ephesus to Rome, where it is affirmed that he was cast into a cauldron of boiling oil. He miraculously escaped without any injury. This supernatural act alarmed Domitian who afterwards banished him to the Isle of Patmos, where he wrote the Book of Revelation. Nerva, the successor of Domitian, recalled him. He was the only apostle who escaped a violent death.

## XVII. Barnabas

He was of Cyprus, but of Jewish descent and his death was supposed to have taken place about AD 73.

It is important to mention that in spite of the harvest of deaths, onslaught of persecutions and horrible punishments, intended to tear the Church of God apart, it daily increased in size and strength. The persecutions and deaths forced the Church to throw itself on the Lord and be deeply rooted in the doctrine of the apostles, and watered constantly and abundantly with the blood of saints.

# Chapter 6. - THE GENERATION OF WICKEDNESS.

1. I receive grace to prevail in prayer in Jesus name.
2. I speak to the stars that in their courses begin to fight against every Sisera in my life in Jesus name.
3. Just as the morning introduces the day, let the sun of glory introduce my glory in God.
4. Every satanic brief of judgment collected on my behalf is today visited with the Holy Ghost fire.
5. In the name of Jesus, I reject every satanic agreement binding my family to disaster, destruction and death
6. I open the door of my life to prosperity, success, health and abundance in Jesus name.
7. I retrieve the keys to my destiny from whosoever is using them to manipulate my life for failure.
8. I register my voice in heaven, so that each time I call heaven may recognize my voice and answer me speedily.
9. I set on fire every satanic case file that carries my name for affliction in Jesus name.
10. O Lord lift up my head among men, just as you did for Joseph in the land of Egypt.

# Chapter Seven
# DEALING WITH THE TROUBLES OF LIFE

*'Man that is born of a woman is of few days; and full of trouble' – Job 14:1*

## *Introduction*

Please recall that in the last chapter, we dealt extensively on the generation of wickedness and how many souls were wasted by powers of darkness. It is important to mention that in spite of the harvest of deaths, onslaught of persecutions and horrible punishments, intended to tear the Church of God apart, it daily increased in size and strength. The persecutions and deaths forced the Church to throw itself on the Lord and be deeply rooted in the doctrine of the apostles, and watered constantly and abundantly with the blood of saints.

It is therefore necessary to know that as you strive for excellence and forge ahead to be signs and wonders, sometimes your experience may prove otherwise. Please do not be discouraged God shall see you through as you lay your hands on the plough. Be encouraged and know you are able. The spirit of God is on the inside, so you can stand up and whip the devil. You however cannot do this in the flesh. God is a spirit and they that must worship him must do it in spirit and truth. We have ready examples in the scriptures of men who confronted the troubles of life headlong and God saw them through.

## *Confronting the troubles of Life*

There was a man with this kind of vision in the Bible called David. He was confronted with a serious problem that affected his family and that of his men. The Amalekites came to Zig-lag and took all of them captives when David and his men went out on a military mission.

> *'And it came to pass when David and his men were come to Zig-lag on the third day, that the Amalekites had invaded the south ...And had taken the women captives. They slew not any either great or small, but carried them away, and went on their ways'*

Let it be clearly known that the Amalekites are all over the place. What is Amalek? Amalek is nothing but the

## DEALING WITH GENERATION WASTERS

flesh. The flesh is always at war with the spirit and the only way to overcome it is to rely on the help of the Holy Spirit. By this means we will not have any condemnation. (Romans 8:1-9).

When the trouble of Zig-lag occurred, David and his people did not know what to do, but to weep before the Lord their God. It was such a distressing moment for him all his armed men and in verse 3 we read that:

*'...David and the people that were with him lifted up their voices and wept.'*

This is the first principle of attaining quick victory. There is a need to weep before the Lord in time of trouble a sign of our helplessness and dependence on him. Our cry is not out of hopelessness but a cry in hope of divine intervention. However, it is important to point out that there are too many dry eyes in the church. It is a pity you do not find men weeping between the porch and the altar these days. Men seem hopeless and helpless with the terrible situation, and therefore resigned to fate. This is one simple reason many are not entering into their inheritance. God desires that we submit ourselves first to him and then resist the devil. (James 4:7)

God is known to be a very present help in time of trouble and has the knowledge of what we go through. When we turn to him we will find answer to our problems. The Bible says that

*'My people perish because they lack knowledge'.*

David wept with his people until they have no more strength to cry. Let us briefly examine the benefit and blessing in weeping before the Lord. In the gospel of Luke Chapter 6 verse 21b we see: '*....Blessed are they that weep now: but ye shall laugh.*'

When will you laugh? In the fullness of times, when your breakthrough is revealed and you come forward to testify to his goodness. This is because

> '*....weeping may endure for a night; but joy cometh in the morning.*' (Ps 30:5)

When the day of Christ comes you shall find joy and peace in him. The day of Christ is not supposed to be the day you are supposed to be weeping. It is a day that you have to tell the devil that you want me to be weeping, in the name of Jesus get out!

In the gospel of Luke Chapter 23 verse 28-31 Jesus told a great company of people that followed him, weep now because the time is coming that you will ask the mountain fall on us and to the hill cover us. This is going to be a terrible time of weeping and gnashing of teeth.

Those that must confront the troubles of life and possess their possession must cry to the Lord to open the heavens for breakthroughs. The Bible reveals that he was in great distress and that '*He cried until he had no strength in him*'. He was greatly distressed because the people planned to stone him to death for the loss of their wives and children. So what did he do in all these? The Bible tells us:

## DEALING WITH GENERATION WASTERS

*' ...but David encouraged himself in the Lord his God.*

A man that must confront the troubles of life and possess his possessions must encourage himself in the Lord. He must convince himself that he is a winner and not a loser. He must never see himself as a failure, but a success that must overcome in time of crisis. He should always say to himself.

**'This mountain that I see I shall see it no more. I will overcome it, because I have Jesus on my side. He defeated the devil, so grace is made available for me to overcome also.'**

The problem of many today is that they are easily discouraged. A young man came to me one time and he said "Sir I am the black sheep of my family" I said "How do you know?" He said 'Because of my experiences.' Then I asked him 'Now what do you want?' He said for me to pray for him to get an American visa. I replied 'Why should I pray such prayer? If you cannot make it here in Nigeria, how are sure you can in America? He kept quiet for a long time and I prayed that the Lord should grant him understanding. I concluded the prayer by asking that the will of the Lord be done.

These are the days when people come to church to give survival testimonies instead of revival testimonies. When they come, they introduce the testimony with long praise the Lord! You hear something like this. 'I have been believing God for my resident permit, but now the Lord has done it praise the Lord'. Now there is nothing wrong with this. But most of the time the truth behind the testimony is concealed. One after the other you hear that of provisions of car, house, life partner, money, promotion, job etc.

You will not hear testimonies such as 'I have been waiting on the Lord for the salvation of my boss for several years. But I wish to testify to the glory of God today, that he is not only saved but baptized in the holy spirit'. You do not hear of people seeking his face for gifts of the spirits but are now operating in them. Neither do you hear testimonies of waiting on God to overcome a dangerous character flaw. No. Revival testimonies are scarce and these speak volume about the foundation or depth of our Christianity today. These people are not better than the gentiles. Mt 6:31 tells us

***'Seek ye first the kingdom of God and his righteousness and all these other things shall follow you'.***

Many go at length to seek these things first and falsify testimonies clinically presented in a way to help God achieve false claims.

Many of us are mundane in ideas and focus. Hence, our thoughts are guided by physical gains than spiritual gains. Christians who are kingdom focused desire more from seeing God fulfilling his goals on earth than man fulfilling his desires. They desire that God's will be done and they bend more to this side. A man that seeks the kingdom of God has these blessings pursuing him.

I knew a brother in Christ, whom I met in one of the house fellowships conducted several years ago. He applied for the American visa and left the handling at the discretion of the embassy. This was after they had collected his relevant papers and consulted with relevant people abroad. He was not desperate. He gave them the information the way it was. They saw his sincerity, against all odds issued him a visa and sent a courier to pursue him with this 'much sought after gold'.

Yet those who juggled their names and out rightly changed their names because their passports have been stamped did not get visa. God is with the upright and stands with them in the day of trouble. As a child of God, you have grace in the place of prayer to ask and you shall receive. You can order the course of your life on your knees and you will see things begin to happen.

Coming back to David, what did he do next? It is important to note the starting point. He did not rely first on his military strength. He chose to turn to the Lord first to guide him on what to do next. He did not intend to go on a wild goose chase, as this would have been the result if he had not considered God first.

He realized it was a hopeless situation except the Lord intervened there would be problem. He refused to think up what to do. There are too many presumptions in the Church today, but David was pragmatic in his approach. The presumptuous Christians can do anything before God ask them to do it. Many have been whipped and flogged by the devil because they did not wait upon the Lord to receive guidance and direction.

The brokenness experienced while weeping before the Lord brought him to a realization of seeking his face for help. David did not waste any more time crying, he took his case before the most high God, the one that could change any situation. He asked for the ephod. This is praying to God in the right spirit and attitude. In I Samuel 30:7-8 we read this account.

*"And David said to Abiathar, Ahimelech's son, I pray thee, bring me hither the Ephod and Abiathar brought hither the Ephod to David. And David enquired from the Lord saying Shall I pursue after this troop? Shall I overtake them? And he answered him, pursue….."*

## *Pursue*

David heard clearly from the Lord, pursue, chase the enemy and cause them to flee. Let the enemy of your life have no rest until you catch up with them and with what they have stolen from you. He gathered the six hundred men that were with him and they went harnessed out of Ziglag in pursuit of the violators of their peace.

In the pursuit of the enemy, there was a major distraction. Out of the six hundred men he had with him two hundred could not continue the pursuit. These men were so weak that he had to leave them behind at

## DEALING WITH GENERATION WASTERS

the brook Besor. (v9, 21). As discouraging as this might be, David was not discouraged. The bible declared ***"But David pursued…."*** (v10). Even though two hundred fell out of the way, David was not deterred. He went ahead with four hundred men still resolute in his conviction that what the Lord had said he was able to bring to pass.

Dear reader, do you get easily discouraged because those with you have fallen aside? Are you distraught with the fact that your former supporters have become weak, that you have been reduced to a lonely voice in the wilderness? Do not worry, God does not save with many, but few, pursue. Do not wait press on till you overcome. Adopt the attitude of the victor and refuse to be a victim. Have a winner mentality and run the race till you catch up with your enemy.

Pursuing is not what you do kneeling down. No you have to mobilize or advance to the center of the battle. You have to take authority. The song 'Pass me not o gentle savior is not a song you sing kneeling down.' While he pursued the enemy his men

***'…found an Egyptian in the field (a servant of an Amalekite) and brought him to David..'*** (I Sam 30:11).

He was sick, left for dead on the way and because he had not eaten for three days and three nights he had no strength in him. His master left him behind to die as he thought this man would have no hope of recovery.

The real issue however was that God sent confusion into their midst, because normally men in this business know that the first principle of survival is that you do not leave any evidence behind. Leaving this man behind was a divine error that led to their being caught. On hearing the good news, David gave orders that the man be fed and when he had eaten he was revived. He was thereafter thoroughly interviewed and he gave vital information as well as promising to take David and his men to his company.

## *OVERTAKE*

It is when men pursue that they can overtake. One thing must lead to the other. Thinking you can overtake and recover all with out making any effort to pursue is the greatest foolhardiness any one could have ever imagined. It is they that put their hands upon the plough and do not look back that fit for the kingdom of God. To overtake, there must be a pursuing and such that even where there is distraction you will not be discouraged.

As they pursued they reduced the gap between them and those that stole all their belongings. They found on the way the Egyptian servant of an Amalekite, whose master left him to die. When the necessary efforts are made the steps to our recovery are assured. As David pursued the words of the Lord kept ringing in his heart:

*'... for thou shall surely overtake them...'*

This gave him assurance that hope was not lost and hence he kept at it.

It is important to note that you need to overtake your enemy in order to remain in control. Yet many people today out of carelessness or in some instances ignorance or weakness allow the enemy to outrun them. The enemy is the one calling the shots, and they dance to the whims and caprices of the overlords. The yoke is in the hand of the enemy and he wields it as he wills. This should not be the case, the devil is supposed to be behind us not in the forefront. In fact, better still he is supposed to be under our feet. This we all know to well but have failed to make the efforts to overcome him. The forefront is for Christ our forerunner, yet through sin we abdicate the throne and easily surrendered to Satan. This is the reason all our prayers are reactionary not actionary.

The devil is allowed to take the initiative, and his victim responds by looking for help to quench his fire. Men have been battered, harassed, intimidated, and oppressed on all points. The hand of the wicked had been so heavy on the Lord's people that, in what seems to be a hopeless situation, the question asked these days is 'What is the devil going to do to me next?'

Yet in the days gone bye, when the disciples of old turned the world upside down the question devil used to ask was 'What is brother John going to do to me next?' Why? The church back then effectively wielded the power of heaven, put the devil to flight and redefined happenings in the heavenly places. They indeed made it clear and real that all power in heaven and on earth had been given to the church.

It is necessary to understand that no matter the pressure you face, no matter the limitations, our God is always a ready answer in time of trouble. There is a promise of God in Isaiah 49:24-26 which assures categorically '*..that the lawful captive can be delivered. ...*' The situation in the church is such that our parents had mortgaged our future at the altar of Satan unknowingly through engaging in seasons of negotiations. Because they do not have relationships with the Lord, they vicariously put some of us into captivity through satanic agreements.

I remember the story of a girl that her parents got her through idolatry. The mother cut a covenant with the powers and fetish sacrifices were made in order to have a child. She was promised a daughter, but the condition attached was that certain rituals must be done before the girl could get married. She conceded to their terms, believed the gods for a baby girl and went home rejoicing.

She indeed got the female child who later grew up to become a believer in Christ. In the fullness of time, God engineered a move to hold a deliverance service where she was to be delivered. As a worker in the children church, it was her portion to bring out the children for prayer and so she did. However, instinctively the man of God laid hand on her without thinking, she fell down with the child to the ground. Immediately, words began to flow: 'You will not die but live, and to declare the glory of the Lord in the land of the living'. That was it God took over from there.

The Thursday before she came for church, her father had put pressure on her to come with him to the fetish priest to carry out the promised rituals that should make her marriage a possibility. She refused and informed her father that she had received the spirit of Christ and hence had been set free from the bondage of Satan. She testified to her father of the power and goodness of the Lord. When somebody receives his conviction through God's revelation, no man can take this away. God confirmed her confession and intervened by delivering her miraculously.

In I Samuel 30:15 we read

*'And David said to him, Canst thou bring me to this company? And he said Swear unto me by God, that thou wilt neither kill me, nor deliver me into the hands of my master, and I will bring you down to this company.'*

The man drew a hard bargain and promised to take David and his men to the enemy location. Even though the bible did not indicate whether David agreed to the man's request but the events that followed corroborated this much. Hence, the time of overtaking and recovering was at hand as David as his men made ready. The man therefore fulfilled his promise

*'And when he had brought him down, Behold, they were spread abroad upon all the earth, eating and drinking, and dancing...'* (v16).

## RECOVER ALL

It is not sufficient to overtake your enemies and when you do what are you going to do with them? These wicked men were rejoicing over the loot they stole from the lands of Judah and the Philistines, when their judgment came. It was so much a time of merry making that they never expected what was about to hit them. Their error of judgment was about to play itself out as the nemesis that was to catch up with them.

Having fulfilled the Lord's instructions to pursue and overtake, and the results seemed favorable David was assured that recovering all would soon be a reality. When David overtook the men, he did not spare any breathing space but he moved sporadically into action and he:

*'...smote them from the twilight even unto the evening of the next day; and there escaped not a man of them...'* (v17)

Just as we witnessed here every recovery is always preceded by warfare. No man takes possession of his possessions from the devil without a fight. It is unthinkable that men would want to achieve this without engaging in a battle; it is like desiring to make omelet without breaking an egg. This is not possible.

There is no place for the lily-livered heart in the art of recovery. Recovery takes diligence, boldness, tact, and resilience. Every weak point must be taken care of so that the devil should not take advantage.

Good news always follows the battle that precedes recovery. Every one that goes to war of a necessity must return to give a testimony of the outcome of the war. The war against the Amalekites would not be an exception and the good news was, just as the Lord said it:

> *'....David recovered all that the Amalekites had carried away: and David rescued his two wives. And there was nothing lacking to them, neither small nor great, neither sons nor daughters, neither spoil, nor anything that they had taken to them: David recovered all'* (I Sam 30:18-19)

## *My Testimony*

For example several years ago, I had to personally pursue the enemy of my life causing hindrance to my progress in life. In 1985 it became apparent that I needed to get a paid employment after my youth service in 1984, if I had to achieve all the goals set before me.

However, I had spent the last quarter of 1984 and the first three quarters of 1985 traveling in respect of the gospel. Several prayer and deliverance ministration trips were made to various places within Nigeria, my home country. Many of us in the team were young men using our time to serve the Lord.

Unknown to me, God was placing me under the tutelage of several men of God to prepare me for future ministry. Combined foundations were laid at the Christian Students Social Movement (CSSM), Nigeria Fellowship of Evangelical Students (NIFES), Ibadan Varcity Christian Union (IVCU) Tuesday Fellowship, (Oshodi, Lagos) and church denominations where I served in various capacities.

While all these lasted, I knew I was not called into full time ministry at that time. So exactly close to a year, I began to call upon the name of the Lord for a job. I challenged God to prove himself as a miracle worker. How could I be preaching faith and it was not working for me? I wish to testify at this point that at the National Youth Service Corps (NYSC) camp, many of my colleagues wrote several applications. In fact there was one who finished 25 envelopes on applications alone! Up until this time I had not written up to two application letters.

In actual fact, I have never written more than two applications for job all my life. Incredible, you may probably say, but that is the truth! The first was to an oil company and the second a computer company where I later worked for twelve years and left as a senior management staff in late 1997.

Sometimes later an opportunity came up for an interview in an oil company. The way and manner in which it happened was not pleasing to me and I knew

## DEALING WITH GENERATION WASTERS

it was not to God either and therefore nothing came out of it. What happened was that my senior brother twisted the hand of one of his friends to field me in on the day of the interview against company rules.

In order to secure my chances I collected letters from some big guys in the society to influence the outcome. Hence, I went about talking about my escapades thereby giving the glory to the creatures rather than the creator. I was so sure the job was mine.

Each time I gave the testimony among brethren, I dropped the names of the big men in government who gave me letters of recommendation. The response was always 'Ah. You do not have problem. Go and relax the job is yours. As soon as the MD sees the letters of those men forget it, you are already in. Congratulations.

But remember us when it is good for you oh!' At the end of the day however, the oil company matter went without any fruit, with all the contacts, and which confirmed that *'Woe is the man that puts his trust in the arm of the flesh.'* (Jer. 17:5). .

Meanwhile, as I was basking in the fallacious glorying of men, God used my brother to draw my attention to an advertisement in the newspaper. Unknown to me this was to be a face-saver from the disappointment that would follow the oil company interview. Can you imagine how merciful our God can be *'His wisdom is past finding out!'*?

Initially I disregarded his counsel and refused to show interest, simply because it was a computer company but he prevailed on me. He took me through several weeks of tutorials on computing to prepare me for the interview. On the interview day, I did so excellently well that I got an ovation on my knowledge of computing.

In spite of the applause at the conclusion of the interview, nothing was heard from the company but I kept praying for God's mercy. I remembered a particular day, in which I prayed from 5.00 a.m. till 11.00 a.m. seeking the Lords intervention for this job. When you are looking for a job or anything dear to your heart, there will always be ample time available to cry unto God.

Just some few minutes after eleven I drifted into a vision half asleep half awake. In it I saw a neighbor of mine three houses away collecting a letter from his friend. The friend told him it is a letter of employment from his company for somebody in the third house. (Brethren, I had never seen this other man before in my life, but when I eventually met him in real life I recognized him immediately. He later became my manager in the office, converted Christian brother, fellowship exco-member, associate and friend in ministry till date.)

As I came back to myself, I prayed and told the Lord to confirm the vision by 12.00 p.m. if he was the one ministering to me. After the prayer I went out to our compound to play table tennis or ping pong. It was a big compound with two giant mango trees. Unknown to me and my siblings the guy at the third house came exactly 12.00 p.m. banging at our gate with nobody to attend to him. It was when he made a return trip in that evening that this revelation came up.

## *DEALING WITH GENERATION WASTERS*

That evening he told me that he was around in the afternoon at 12.00 p.m. to inform my sister of the employment they gave her in a computer company. The reason he concentrated on my sister was the fact that he was interested in her and he found the information as a veritable ground to play his game. But unfortunately for him I hinted him the message was for me, oh how disappointed he was on this matter!

However, it is important to mention that the devil will fight to the end whatever God has promised to do in your life. On hearing the information he gave me, I started to testify to the goodness of the Lord. You can then imagine my shock, when after about six days, this man came back to inform me that his friend made a mistake. Right down in my spirit I knew the devil was up to a trick. He gave this information to me right in the middle of my grand mother's burial party. He ruined that day for me, as I had no more strength in me to entertain my friends. As far as I was concerned it was a call to prayers.

I went straight into my room and praised God all night - thanking him for what he had done. The first person to call on me on the fateful Saturday morning was a pastor friend of mine. He immediately picked the weight on my spirit and got me to relay to him the information I got the night before. He asked me what do you want. I told him I wanted the letter of employment to arrive on Monday. He said 'Let us agree for Friday' but later changed his mind for Monday. We prayed a prayer of agreement and trusted the Lord. However, the letter did not come on Monday.

In spite of this situation I trusted the Lord. While I was at the fellowship on Tuesday, a word of prophecy came confirming that God had blessed a brother but the devil is fighting hard to stop it. I knew that was for me and I told my cousin as soon as the fellowship ended. This word from God strengthened my faith and I began aggressive thanksgiving unto God.

Eventually on Friday morning, as I was rounding up my morning prayers I heard a chorus of rejoicing in the living room. 'Praise the Lord it has arrived! It has come! Glory be to God'. The loudest of the voices was my cousin's, who was with me at the fellowship. The whole family had been monitoring the letter both spiritually and physically. The spirit of God told me, as the holy commotion was on that your letter of employment has arrived.

Brethren, there is nothing prayer cannot do. The man who was supposed to hand deliver the letter to me, confessed several years after as we were having a tête-à-tête during break in the office how he got to the street next to our own and got tired, hence decided to post the last letter with him - which incidentally was mine. It was a great offence in those days to post letter in that company. It must be hand delivered or mailed through a Courier Company. These were the days in which bags of letters were tampered with but God preserved mine and I got it. His confirmation made me to thank God the more and came to understand the workings of prayer, praise the Lord.

# Chapter 7 – DEALING WITH THE TROUBLES OF LIFE

1. O Lord! Let my light so shine that my enemies will be the ones to advertise my blessings.

2. O Lord! Let my life be so aglow that the people may be drawn to the glory of my rising.

3. O Lord! In your mercy gather me for blessings in Jesus name.

4. Make me a cup of poison unto all the people that have laid siege against my soul.

5. O Lord Make me a burdensome stone unto all that wish to carry me about into destruction.

6. O Lord Make me a burdensome stone unto all that carry my story about and let them be cut to pieces.

7. O Lord! Smite every satanic and oppressive horse of my life with astonishment by giving me victory over it.

8. I Smite the rider with madness as you give me power to overcome them.

9. Watch over me and deliver me from my oppressors.

10. O Lord !Just as the fish that swallowed Jonah vomited him, let all the troubles of life that had swallowed me vomit me now.

# Chapter Eight
# TAKE DOMINION

*'.. When God bringeth back the captivity of his people, Jacob shall rejoice, and Israel shall be glad'- Ps. 53:6*

## *Divine Secrets Against Wasters*

The bible informs us in Psalm 84 about the secret of building up strength against the powers of darkness. It is crucial to recognize: *'How amiable are thy tabernacles, O Lord of hosts!'* (v1). The house of God must be inviting and attractive to one in such a way that one desires it like David. When this is one's strong persuasion, the first level of battles over the kingdom of darkness is won. This is simply because the man with such persuasion is blessed and he shall:

*'...be satisfied with the goodness of thy house, even of thy holy temple.'* (Ps 65:4)

The man dwelling in God's house shall long for the courts of the Lord that is the place of prayer. This in itself attracts its own blessing. The bible informs us that

> *'Blessed is the man whom thou choosest, and causest to approach unto thee, that he may dwell in thy courts:...'* (Ps 65:4).

Why is the man blessed? It is because he has access to divine secrets in God's court. It is in this place that his heart and flesh cry out for the living God.

Verse 4 of this Psalm reechoes the fact that the man that dwells in the house of God is blessed and *'..they will be still praising thee.'* This simply means they will continue to have reasons to testify to God because of his faithfulness and goodness all the time. This is also because they have located their place on God's altar (v3). This was indeed the desire of David and those who desire the same thing from God and will pray the prayer of David in Ps 43:3-4 in order to be ushered into divine revelation.

> *'O send out thy light and thy truth: let them* (light and truth) *lead me; and let them* (light and truth) *bring me unto thy holy hill* (the place of prayer), *and to thy tabernacles* (temple). *Then will I go unto the altar of God, .....'*

The altar is a place of blessing and contact with God of heaven. One receives divine protection on his altar. In addition, we are told that:

***'Blessed is the man whose strength is in thee: in whose heart are the ways of them. Who passing through the valley of Baca make it a well; the rain also filled the pools.'*** (v5-6).

These men have the mind of those who do the impossible or turn impossible situations around. A valley without water became a well springing with water and they also prayed rain down upon the dry ground. These men the bible tells us grow from strength to strength because ***'..everyone of them in Zion appeareth before God.'*** (v7) in continuous prayer warfare.

## *The Only Guarantee For Protection Is Prayer*

It is only continuous watch in prayer that guarantees protection against generation wasters. When one consistently hides in the secret place of the most high, God he shall abide under the shadow of his wings. Even though he walks through the valley of the shadow of death nothing shall happen to him. This is because in committing himself constantly to prayers, he has the Lord as his trust and shield. (refs: Ps 91:1; Ps 23:4)

The enemy is always out there looking for whom to devour, hence the bible warns us to watch and pray. One is indeed powerless and hopeless without prayers when confronted by this evil force of darkness. Their operation is so deadly that nothing of the person is left after they finished with him. One can understand the implication of why the writer of Joel advised that the old men and the inhabitants of the land should pass the gruesome message of happenings in their times to their children and,

> *'.. and let your children tell their children, and their children another generation'* (Joel 1:3).

The reason was to warn them to be watchful less they are confronted with similar problems in life. The account of happening was so terrible that three great army of eaters or agents of destruction came together to demonstrate their prowess at destruction. It was so bad that it was clinical destruction so much so that we read in Joel 1:4 that:

> *"That which the palmerworm hath left hath the locust eaten; and that which the locust hath left hath the cankerworm eaten; and that which the cankerworm hath left hath the caterpillar eaten"*

Each destroyer has its area of specialization and after dealing with the victim to its maximum limits handed him or her over to the next. And of course the last agent in action, the caterpillar left nothing of its victim after dealing with it. It was destruction per excellence. At the end of the day the post mortem report of the actions of these agents are quoted:

> *"He hath laid my vine waste, and barked my fig tree: he hath made it clean bare, and cast*

*it away; the branches thereof are made white.* v7,

*"The field is wasted, the land mourneth; for the corn is wasted: the new wine is dried up, the oil languisheth."* v10.

May the Lord open our eyes and help us to overcome the evils set against our life in Jesus name. This is because these powers of destruction ruined the promising Demas and wasted Judas Iscariot through lust and greed. With God on our side however there is always a way out for those who are willing to cast all their cares upon him and ask for his mercies before it is too late. These are those who are not willing to observe lying vanities, because

*'They that observe lying vanities forsake their own mercy.'* (Jonah 2:8).

Everyone uniquely has a measure of mercy ordained for him by God to rescue him in time of trouble. However, if such a person trusts in the arm of the flesh, riches, horoscope, or fetish powers etc he forsakes his own measure of mercy. Nothing that has been broken to pieces is beyond God to put together, because He is the solution center. All one needs do is to seek him and one will find him. He is willing to hear the cry of the oppressed and arise on their behalf. When he does he shall fulfill his promise as mentioned in the book of Joel Chapter 2 in verse 25-26.

*"And I will restore to you the years that the locust hath eaten, the cankerworm, and the caterpillar, and the palmerworm, my great army which I sent among you."*

*And ye shall eat in plenty, and be satisfied, and praise the name of the Lord your God, that hath dealt wondrously with you: and my people shall never be ashamed'*

## Dealing With The Gates of Hell

How will the promise of Joel be fulfilled? It is salient to know that the empowerment associated with salvation is the beauty attached to becoming a child of God. As children called to be saints, we are also spiritual soldiers enlisted into the army of God. Therefore, our operation is not physical but spiritual. The intention of God is that the army of God, the Church, shall fight in the last day's battle against the forces of darkness.

To achieve this purpose the Lord Jesus Christ has done everything possible to prepare and position this army for battle. In fact, he personally drew the attention of the world to this standing army by declaring in the gospel of Mathew chapter 16 verse 18 that:

*"I will build my church and the gates of hell shall not prevail against it"*

This is nothing but an open challenge against the enemy and also a challenge to the Church to remain prepared

## DEALING WITH GENERATION WASTERS

for contention when the need arises. The obvious need to be ready for unexpected battle and also the assurance of being victorious over the enemy are implied. That the Church of Jesus must by necessity be in dominion is not negotiable. If the gates of hell therefore should not prevail against it, the Church must be battle ready.

This been the case, the Church must engage itself with unrelenting and aggressive spiritual warfare. This becomes salient because, the way the devil is killing, stealing, and destroying makes even the strong hearted to become apprehensive. The wise ones in the Church know that the battle of the last days requires no notice at all. It shall come upon the unsuspecting victim suddenly like a thief in the night.

There is no doubt that the signs for the battle of the last days are upon us and we must be ready to fight in order to be in dominion. Whether you want to believe it or not, the truth brethren is that we must fight. Our Lord and Master have already made the call to battle. So be ready to take the battle to the very gates of the enemy.

Do not allow the enemy to take the initiative. You must constantly initiate sporadic assault against the enemy of your life. No excuses anymore because it is time to rise up and confront the enemies at your gates with unexpected violence or surprise attack. Let him not have any breathing space to recover strength. Pummel him to submission and ride into the kingdom with shouts of triumph. Trust the Lord to help you in times like this. Do not be intimidated by the devil's psychological warfare. The righteous is as bold as a Lion. Give no room to fear, you can do it.

## Obey God's Command

The Lord is a man of war and He is to lead the Church in the last days' battle against the Kingdom of darkness. In order to achieve this, it is important to articulate the instruction of the Lord in the book of Genesis. When the decision to make man was to be effected it was with a definite purpose in God's mind. This purpose was specified clearly in Genesis Chapter 1 verse 26:

> *'....let them have dominion over the fish of the sea, and over the fowl of the air, and over the cattle, and over all the earth, and over every creeping thing that creepeth upon the earth.'*

Man was therefore created to be in dominion over his environment. He is to be God's man on ground. This however, cannot be possible except man abides in Him and dwells in His presence. The build up of fellowship with Him would result in trusting in Him and this should equip man for battle. Submission to God also has its role in the matter. Dominion cannot be achieved except a man submits to Him. He will glorify Himself through us only if we allow Him to do so. As we pray, trust and obey we exercise dominion through Him.

He watches over us in every battle and is willing to grant us victory as we move out in faith. He makes power and fire available for us to do exploits. The exploits in turn are to convert the kingdoms of this world unto the kingdoms of our Lord and of his Christ. God has put a lot of premium on man. He desires a man to work with especially in the place of prayer. The prayer life of a man affects the happenings in heaven and on earth. This fact, spiritually articulate men who are knowledgeable in the art of spiritual warfare know very well.

These are tested men in battle. They are men that stand with the Lord by night in prayer. They sincerely know the importance of such prayers and the implication or danger of not doing so. Since witches and wizards operate mostly at night these men offer their sleep as sacrifices to deal with the operations of darkness. This is to ensure the progress of God's work as well as the peace of the people on the earth, because it is:

*".... while men slept, his enemy came and sowed tares among the wheat, and went his way.'* (Mt 13:25).

These men walk so closely with God that they are called saviors in the book of Obadiah verse 21:

*"And saviours shall come up on mount Zion to judge the mount of Esau: and the kingdom shall be the Lord's."*

They are also deliverers who have come to understand that for every mountain of Zion there is a mount of Esau to contend with.

## Dominion Over The Land

The powers of darkness cannot operate, if men do not give them access into their lives. These powers control different geographical spheres of influence. That is why for every king that sits upon the throne, there is a spiritual duplicate that actually rules.

The fight for the possession of the land had been on for a long time. It was the same reason why Satan beguiled Eve to have the controlling influence over the earth. As if this was not enough, he tempted the Lord Jesus to bow unto him and he would give him the world. The land is paramount to the kingdom of darkness that the forces of wickedness have done everything to maintain control over it.

In the book of Exodus, Chapter 7 from verse 9 we see God's strategic counsel to Moses in order to exercise dominion over the land of Egypt.

*'When Pharaoh shall speak unto you, saying, shew a miracle for you: then thou shalt say unto Aaron, Take thy rod, and cast it before Pharaoh, and it shall become serpent.*

The Bible records that both Moses and Aaron carried out the Lord's instruction to the letter. It is important to highlight the fact that they *'...went in unto Pharaoh...'* (v10). This is the way we need to go in and confront the problems we face in life. No matter how strong or tough the enemy may be, it is very important that we go in after him and challenge him in the name of Jesus.

## DEALING WITH GENERATION WASTERS

When they got to Pharaoh's presence Aaron cast down his rod and it became a serpent (v10). One may begin to wonder why serpent? Please recall that in Genesis Chapter 3 that it was the serpent that took over dominion from man and usurped man's authority through subtlety.

> *'Now the serpent was more subtil than any beast of the field which the Lord God had made...'*
> (Gen. 3:1).

Adam had given the land to it on a platter of gold at his fall. So everywhere the land is in contention the serpent is there to rise in protest. When the hedge over the land is broken a serpent will bite. This also holds true if authority is not exercised over the land and the ruling powers over it.

> *'Surely the serpent will bite without enchantment*
> (or without taking authority)..' (Eccl. 10:11).

Going back to Pharaoh's palace, what happened after Aaron's rod became a serpent. Pharaoh was not in any way intimidated by what he saw, because he was on familiar terrain. Scenarios like this would have been created hitherto, in the palace through magic and sorcery. He was so sure of this that with confidence he

> *'..called his wise men and the sorcerers;...*(who) *did in like manner with their enchantments'*
> (v11).

This act of affront helped to harden the heart of Pharaoh that there was nothing to it. Even when

*'..Aaron's rod swallowed up their rods'* he was not in any way moved. This battle was significant because God's victory here symbolizes dominion over the land. Even though victory over the land had been achieved, Pharaoh looked up to another source of contact with spiritual power. Apart from the fact that God hardened his heart, the assurance of contact with alternative spiritual power source, was one of the reasons why he was not troubled.

## *Dominion Over The Water*

While God hardened his heart he was waiting on the sideline to deal with Pharaoh's alternative with dispatch. Victory in spiritual warfare largely depends on one's ability to hear from God or take advantage of revelation from God. This is a key factor in achieving victory in spiritual warfare. Revelation is the quick access key to victory over perceived enemy.

While Moses and Aaron were basking in the joy of victory, Pharaoh was planning his counter attack outside the influence of the abilities of his once humiliated magicians and sorcerers. The Lord in reiterating the fact of Pharaoh's evil plan made Moses to realize that his heart is hardened and was willing to do all that was in his power to ensure that *'…he refuseth to let the people go'.* (v14).

The Lord therefore revealed to Moses in the next verse the strategy to adopt to counter pharaoh's plan.

## DEALING WITH GENERATION WASTERS

*'Get thee unto Pharaoh in the morning; lo, he goeth out unto the water; and thou shalt stand by the river's brink against he come;…..'*

Ordinarily, one may argue the fact that Pharaoh was going to the waters to wash, but looking deeply into God's command should give one a rethink

*'..thou shalt stand by the river's brink against he come;…..'*

In simple interpretation, you must get to the river before Pharaoh gets there and wait there until he comes.

In addition, God instructed him

*'..and the rod which was turned to a serpent shalt thou take in thy hand.'* (v15b)

The rod had been a rod of witness of God's victory over the power on the land. It was Moses' symbol of authority or staff of office. All Pharaoh's magicians and sorcerers had lost their authority to the authority of God. This rod Pharaoh must see again and witnessed as the authority through which the man of God exercised dominion.

Why were these instructions very crucial? One may not indeed make anything of it until one gets to understand the motive of Pharaoh as we read the book of Ezekiel, Chapter 29. Just as there is a physical Pharaoh, there is also a spiritual one that ruled with him on the throne. He was therefore going into the waters for consultations with the spiritual power source in the waters. We thank

God who had instructed that the Son of man should set his face against Pharaoh and Egypt and say:

*'..I am against thee, Pharaoh King of Egypt, the great dragon that lieth in the midst of his rivers...'* (v3).

This same Pharaoh the Bible tells us he is *'..a whale in the seas..'* (Ezk 32:2) and *'The waters made him great...'* (Ezk 31:4). He had acquired so much power that he had assumed possession of the creation of God. The book of Ezekiel 29:3 expresses his audacity and the ascription of God's creation to himself when it reveals that he:

*'...hath sad, My river is mine own, and I have made it for myself.'*

That powers under the waters have caused havoc against humanity is a well-known fact. Agents of marine spirits turn people's hearts away from God create evil or deadly things. When you think about the way men and women craze for societal trends that add little or no value to life you begin to wonder why. Both old and young, married and single, believers and unbelievers compete without shame for recognition in this world of sin not knowing they are all under the influence of marine spirits.

It is a known fact that fashion trends, beauty articles such as jewelry, clothes, shoes, creams, shampoos, lip sticks, nail polish and vanish, nail extenders, wigs, hairdos etc are designs heavily influenced by water spirits. No wonder the book of Job 26 verse 5 declares that

*'Dead things are formed from under the waters...'*

In addition, they have through television and personal contacts influenced many to the point in which they have resolved to go out half-naked in the name of fashion. Many have lost respect for modesty that they wear clothes that expose all and leave very little to imagination. Our campuses and some of our churches are places, for example, where these spectacles of shame are demonstrated without battling an eye.

Now back to the action spot where Moses was given divine instruction to act. The need for Moses to take the rod with him was very pertinent because, there was a Pharaoh a great dragon lying in the midst of his rivers that must be dealt with. What was he to do with the rod? God needed him to neutralize the authority of the power under the water by using the rod to cause the blood of the lamb to fill the waters and destroy the great dragon lying in it. As Moses and Aaron carried out God's instructions, the bible informs us that:

*'..all the waters that were in the river were turned to blood. And the fish that was in the river died;..'* (v20-21)

Apart from the dragon that lies in the midst of the river, the frog was also another collaborating entity that must be dealt with in order to put an end to the psychic powers of Pharaoh and his magicians. In Exodus chapter 8 verses 5-7 we saw God through Moses and Aaron move against frogs in the waters.

> *'And the Lord spake unto Moses, say unto Aaron, Stretch forth thine hand with thy rod over the streams, over the rivers and over the ponds and cause frogs to come up upon the land of Egypt.'* (v5).

Why were the frogs called out of the waters? The waters symbolize their strength and a fish out of water is helpless and hopeless. So God through his servant called them out of the waters to die

> *'...out of the houses, out of the villages, and out of the fields.'* (v14).

As mentioned earlier, God organized their mass destruction and burial for a purpose. This was to conclusively deal with the combinative deadly potency of the dragon and the frogs in the land of Egypt. These two are powers that *'..go forth unto the kings of the earth..'* (Rev 16:14) to give them undue advantage over the control of men's lives.

These two have empowered and engineered sorcery and magic in kings' palaces. This the Bible in Revelation 16 verses 13-14 confirms as

> *'..unclean spirits like frogs come out of the mouth of the dragon...'*

If you remember the revelation of Pharaoh in the book Ezekiel Chapter 29 *'..the great dragon that lieth in*

## DEALING WITH GENERATION WASTERS

*the midst of his river'* this will become clear to you. The dragon emits the unclean spirits like frogs to wrath evil influence over humanity. What do both of them represent? The frog and dragon are symbols of satanic power working lying miracles. This is confirmed in Revelation 16 verses 13-14 that:

*'...they are the spirits of devils, working miracles...'*

Armed with this information, it should not therefore be far from you to piece together the reason why after this the magicians and sorcerers of Pharaoh could no more perform miracles. At the instruction of God, after dealing with the frogs, Aaron:

*'..stretched out his hand with his rod, and smote the dust of the earth, and it became lice in man, and in beasts;...'* (Ex 8:17).

The Bible gives a vivid account in verse 18 of how:

*'..the magicians did so with their enchantments to bring forth lice..'*

The verdict on this attempt was that *'..they could not...'* Why could they not? It was because the spirit of frogs and dragon working miracles had been dealt with and dominion had been achieved over the waters just in the same way Jesus walked on water (Mk 6:46-51)

In the final analyses total dominion over the powers and consequent overthrow of Pharaoh in the waters fulfilled the words of God through Prophet Ezekiel and sealed the dominion of God through Moses over the waters.

> *'But I will put hooks in thy jaws, and I will cause the fish of thy rivers to stick unto thy scales, and I will bring thee up out of the midst of thy rivers, and all the fish of thy rivers shall stick unto thy scales.*
>
> *And I will leave thee thrown into the wilderness, thee and all the fish of thy rivers: thou shalt fall upon the open fields: thou shalt not be brought together, nor gathered: I have given thee for meat to the beasts of the field and to the fowls of the heaven.'* (Ezek. 29:4-5)

The above prophecy is a confirmation that God desires that we have dominion and be in order for us to ensure the prophecy above become the lot of the Pharaoh in our lives. The book of Exodus Chapter 14 verses 27-30 lucidly draws our attention to what should be the constant refrain written concerning our Pharaohs:

> *'...and the Lord overthrew the Egyptians in the midst of the sea. ..and Israel saw the Egyptians dead upon the sea shore.'*

So shall it be concerning your enemies in Jesus mighty name. Amen.

## Dominion Over The Heavens

That the battle of the last days' would significantly be the battle fought through the help of God in the heavenly places cannot be overemphasized. It is going to be the battle of gods. Just like current world strategy for full-scale war is based on the combination of the air force's massive aerial strikes, the navy's provision of aircraft carrier for take off and landing operations and land army's move in for mop up operation. The end time battle shall be thus strategic.

The survival of a Christian in the end time will largely depend on the level at which he can operate in warfare. It is not just a question of binding and losing. The present situation requires strategic level warfare, where the one praying has deep knowledge of the power he is dealing with. He must be able to shake the heavens, the sea and the earth. The strategic location of the forces warring against him must be located and liquidated. It is not an accident of words when the Holy Spirit declared in Haggai Chapter 2 verse 6 that:

*'..Yet once, it is a little while, and I will shake the heavens, and the earth, and the sea, and the dry land.'*

The fulfillment of the above words is so significant that it would determine a lot of things in the realm of the spirit. When all the shake-able are achieved it would produce wonderful result. The verse following it beautifully confirms the benefit awaiting the people if these things are shaken. It is then that *'...the desire*

***of all nations shall come:..'*** All aborted or stillborn desires would receive instant fulfillment and men should enter into their inheritances.

We see this playing itself out beautifully in the case of Moses/Aaron versus Pharaoh in the book of Exodus. One of the strategies God reserved to deal with Pharaoh was the shaking of the heavens. The problems of Pharaoh and his men became compounded when they could no more perform miracles through the spirit of frogs. All the plagues God released against Egypt from that moment could no more be replicated. It was from that point one sided, no match contest. The battle was sore against them that the magicians confessed to Pharaoh in Exodus 8:19 that ***'..This is the finger of God...'***. If his finger could do that much damage, just imagine what his hand would do!

In every situation, the Lord we serve is always ahead of the enemy. He sees the beginning from the end and sees the end from the beginning. Even before the encounter with Pharaoh was to be executed, he had released prophetic words ahead of the time. These words were to take care of happenings at that particular time. God incubated those words in the heavens. These were the words that finished the one who depended on the arm of the flesh to fight.

> ***'Woe unto them that go down to Egypt for help; and stay on horses, and trust in chariots, because they are many, and in horsemen, because they are very strong; but they look not unto the Holy One of Israel, neither seek the Lord!'***

## DEALING WITH GENERATION WASTERS

Why is it that the Bible says 'Woe unto them,,'? It is simply because that is the portion of everyone that puts his trust in the arm of the flesh. That man is under a curse as Jeremiah 17:5 confirms. The flesh begets the flesh, while the spirit begets the things of the spirit. It is hopeless to assume that the strength of the flesh will suffice in the day of battle against spiritual forces. This is the reason why going to seek help in Egypt (the world) is foolishness. Worldly help only procures disappointment and disaster because:

*'Now the Egyptians are men, and not God; and their horses flesh and not spirit. When the Lord shall stretch out his hand, both he that helpeth shall fall, and he that is holpen shall fall down, and they all shall fail together.'* (Isaiah 31:1, 3)

In the book of Ezekiel Chapter 30 verse 18 we read the frightening prophetic declaration of God against Egypt.:

*'At Tehaphnehes also the day shall be darkened, when I shall break there the yokes of Egypt...'*

This for Egypt would be a day of thick darkness when people would grope in darkness in daytime as if it was night. God was to deal with the power bases of Egypt in the heavens. He put forth a notice to the elements in the heavens that he was going to deal with them:

*'And when I shall put thee out, I will cover the heaven, and make the stars thereof dark; I will*

*cover the sun with a cloud, and the moon shall not give her light.' (Ezk. 32:7)*

The zodiac signs and all it stood for were to be tampered with in order to silence the gods. The words incubated in the sun, moon and the stars were to be wiped out. All the satanic information databank was to be made nonsense of by the superior power of heaven. The sun, moon, and the stars would lose the ability to give light temporarily because of divine interjection:

*'All the bright lights of heaven will I make dark over thee, and set darkness upon thy land, saith the Lord god.'* (v8)

Was the Lord able to carry out this threat? Of course he did for a specific period of days, which symbolized the power of the trinity as we read in Exodus Chapter 10 verse 22:

*'And Moses stretched forth his hand toward heaven; and there was thick darkness in all the land of Egypt for three days:'*

The above was paralyzing darkness in such a way that the elements were suspended in fulfilling the function of telling the seasons for three days while the darkness lasted. While there was darkness in Egypt there was light in the land of Goshen.

God wiped off the words incubated in the heavenly bodies and made nonsense of the powers of Egypt. He proved his dominion over the heavens and made mockery of their sun god, moon goddess, and all Egypt stood for. No matter what you believe, God is God and in him alone is divine strength and help.

## *Rise Up And Take Dominion*

It is about time you woke up from inactivity, and map out your strategy for the takeover of every portion of ground the enemy uses to oppress you. Let your former obstacles be the raw materials for your miracle. Create the platform for God to stand upon when he arises through your prayers, because this shall prove to be the beginning of the scattering of your enemies.

God is waiting for you to take the initiative. Make the first move and let God grant you strength for dominion as he had promised. He will also equip you for continuous victory over your enemy. It is when you release yourself that this promise becomes operational. Turn to him and ask for His help, He is willing to help you.

The decision to succeed lies squarely with you. Present yourself for the renewal of power and strength. God will release the necessary anointing to make this a reality. When this happens every yoke shall be destroyed and you shall be set free from captivity. You shall sing with the shout of triumph in the name of Jesus.

# Chapter 8 – **TAKE DOMINION**

1. I receive divine help for dominion as I pray in Jesus name.

2. Let the covering clothes of the wicked narrow so that they will be consumed by 0 degrees cold.

3. Let their bed too short for them to lie on.

4. I whet my tongue like a sword, so that as I rebuke the enemies of my life let them be cut to pieces.

5. I cut in pieces through spoken word every satanic rope used to tie me down in Jesus name.

6. Let the arrows of the Lord wound my enemy so that they will lift off their hands from my case.

7. I set on fire every satanic case file that carries my name or that of any member of my family.

8. You forces of limitation, I command you go now.

9. Spirit of the living God let me be a magnet that will attract good things of life to myself.

10. O Lord! I decree that my life attract blessing, success, victory and breakthroughs today in Jesus name.

# Chapter Nine
# POSSESSING YOUR POSSESSIONS

*'But upon mount Zion there shall be deliverance, there shall be holiness and the house of Jacob shall possess their possessions'- Obadiah 18*

## *Introduction*

One of the reasons a man must take dominion over the affairs of his life is the need to possess his possessions. It is clear from the scriptures that one's desire may not be realizable except violence is ministered to the devil. He only understands the language of force, and he that is unwilling to apply force against the entities of darkness may die prematurely. He will hear about good things of life kept in store for him and will never live to enjoy it. Such a person will die in servitude.

This is one reason we are looking at the need to possess your possessions. I have come to realize that there are many people in the church who lack the understanding of where we started. It is important to note that any one that must possess his possessions must be militant. The kingdom of God suffers violence and the violent ones take it by force. Many opportunities in life have been buried by agents of darkness because of lack of aggressive approach of the people involved. Many things have been taken for granted; hence the enemy is calling the shots.

The Lord established the fact of our militancy when he mentioned that I will build my church and the gates of hell shall not prevail against it. Contrary to the desire and injunction of Christ, there are many beggars in church. They beg the devil to leave them alone, they beg God to deliver them, and beg man for help. But God has given us power over all principalities and powers and he expects us to go ahead and deal with them. God has no apologies for the devil. He said in Mathew 8:18

***'Whatsoever you bind on earth, shall be bound in heaven; and whatsoever you loose on earth shall be loosed in heaven'***

Even though the Bible confirms the availability of grace given to man to overcome the powers of darkness, many have refused to tap into it. We want to be free on our own terms, without having to pay the price of spending time in God's presence. Little time spent in God's presence results in little power. Man cannot be much for God, if he does not spend much time in prayer. Prayer opens one's eye to see the benefits available to those that are yielded to God. The ability of God is available to make one a winner in the battles of life because:

*'.. greater is he that is in you than he that is in the world'.* (I Jn 4:4)

## *The Generation of Christ*

The fact that greater is the one that is in us speaks clearly of God's empowerment from on high. All we desire to fulfill God's calling and mandate are available in us. The Lord died that we may die and resurrect with him. He brought us forth by his death and resurrection. It is clear in the Bible that we are the generation of Christ. A cursory look at the gospel of Mathew Chapter 1 verse 17 reveals this much and there we read the following words

*"So all the generations and from Abraham unto David are fourteen generations, from David unto the carrying away unto Babylon are fourteen generations and from the Babylon unto the carrying away to Christ are fourteen generations.'*

When all the generations are added together you have forty-two. However, on individual count you will discover that Joseph the foster father of Jesus is number forty, our Lord, Jesus is number forty-one. Who then is the forty-second generation?

It is important to take a closer look into the Bible, and study the account of David on the revelation God gave him about the Lord and his anointed ones in the book of Psalms Chapter 2 verses 1-2 in order to answer this question.

> *'Why do the heathen rage, and the people imagine a vain thing?*
>
> *The kings of the earth set themselves, and the rulers take counsel together against the Lord, and against his anointed,..'*

It is equally pertinent to compare the reference of Apostle Peter to these same verses quoted in Acts of the Apostles Chapter 4 verses 25-26. In rendering these verses, Apostle Peter through the help of the Holy Spirit introduced an eye opener, as to whom the anointed ones referred to in Psalm 2 verse 2 are.

> *'Who by the mouth of thy servant David hast said, Why did the heathen rage, and the people imagine vain things?*
>
> *The kings of the earth stood up, and the rulers were gathered together against the Lord, and against his Christ.'*

In analyzing both references, two words meaning the same thing came up for observation. While the words of David revealed that they gathered *'..against the Lord, and against his anointed,...'*; that of Peter mentioned that they gathered '..*against the Lord, and against his Christ.'*

We are aware from the scriptures that it is a curse if a man does not bring forth. We saw this curse automatically manifest in the life of Judas Iscariot because of the role he played in the crucifixion of Jesus. There was no account of his ever bringing forth any child because of the prophetic curse that he brought upon himself. We find an affirmation of these curses in the Psalms of David Chapters 69 verse 25 and 109 verse 8 (Also ref: Acts 1:20).

*'Let their habitation be desolate; and let none dwell in their tents'* and *'let another take his office'*

Being aware of the above fact, Prophet Isaiah began a lamentation on the Lord Jesus about his generation. He was deeply concerned about his early death and not known to have physically brought forth children. As a result he asked this question: "*...Who shall declare his generation?'* (Is. 53:8). What Isaiah was saying in effect is 'Who is going to reveal his children now that '*..he was cut off out of the land of the living?'*

We thank God that the Holy Spirit has an insight into the way and manner the Lord would bring forth. While the lamentation lasted, the spirit of prophecy picked the mind of God on the way and manner in which the seed (children) of Christ was to come. That is the generation that ought to be declared. Hence we read in verse 10 of the same chapter these words:

> *'Yet it pleased the Lord to bruise him... when thou shalt make his soul an offering for sin, he shall see his seed..'*

It is indeed comforting to know that the Lord Jesus indeed brought forth through his death and resurrection. He must die for his children to be revealed. His death and resurrection was to be the womb through which the children were to be borne and brought forth. The above revelation confirms what David and Apostle Peter commented about respectively on the Lord and his anointed or Christ. It is clear that the word *'anointed'* is the same word translated *'Christ'* by the Holy Spirit through Peter.

Now, let us go back to the Gospel of Mathew Chapter 1 verse 17 again. Recall that earlier on it was mentioned that when all the generations are added together you have forty-two. And that on individual count you will discover that Joseph the foster father of Jesus is number forty, our Lord, Jesus is number forty-one. The question still waiting to be answered is who then is the forty-second generation?

When you closely look at the verse in reference, it states in the closing reference

> *' ...and from the carrying away into Babylon unto Christ are fourteen generations.'*

If Joseph was 40, Jesus 41 then his seed is 42. This therefore confirms that the word *'Christ'* is a reference to the anointed ones brought forth by Jesus. These are

## DEALING WITH GENERATION WASTERS

simply the seed or fruit of the Lord Jesus Christ (the anointed) or better put the Church.

Apostle Paul took us into a deeper dimension on this subject. He picked the matter up from the promise God made to Abraham concerning Isaac and convincingly proved to the reader that Isaac was a type of that seed. The seed, which is Christ is God's ultimate goal.

The Lord Jesus reconciled all things to himself by the blood of his cross. Notice the reference of Apostle Paul and how he interchangeably used the words *'seed'* and *'Christ'* in Chapter 3:verse 16 of the Epistle to the Galatians:

*'Now to Abraham and his seed were the promises made. He saith not, And to seeds, as of many; but as of one, And to thy seed, which is Christ.'*

King David in the book of Psalms, in the same manner even made a stronger statement in Chapter 22 verse 30 that:

*'A seed shall serve him: it shall be accounted to the Lord for a generation.'*

Notice also that, it is a seed, but that seed will be reckoned after the name of the Lord for a generation! The generation that his seed shall serve him and also be accounted to him is the 42$^{nd}$ generation.

It is clear from the verse above that this seed is raised to serve and it is the body of Christ revealed. This seed shall minister righteousness to the blind and lost. They shall be the Lord's witnesses in Jerusalem, Judea, Samaria, and the uttermost part of the earth. They shall not be idle seed, but the seed that will be effective and equally efficient in the service of the Lord. This fact is affirmed in verse 31 and they:

*'.... shall come, and declare his righteousness unto a people that shall be born, that he hath done this.'*

Of course, it is quite clear that one does not use *'they'* for a person. The word *'they'* is a reference to multitudes of people – that is '*.......the generation of them that seek him, that seek thy face, O Jacob'.* They will stand by night in the house of the Lord and lift up their faces to heaven in great expectation. They shall not only be a people of prayer, but houses of prayer unto the Lord. They shall cry between the porch and the altar, and the Lord shall hear them.

I want you to understand that this generation we are talking about shall not only serve and pray, they shall also be people of praise. This chosen generation shall distinctively manifest this grace to the emulation of others. The book of Psalms chapter 102 verse 18 prophetically declares that:

*'This shall be written for the generation to come, the people that shall be created shall praise the Lord.*

It is important to clarify the words *'the people that shall be created'*. Who are these people in reference and what creation is the Holy Spirit speaking about? Let it be clear in your mind that these people are those saved and sanctified. This verse is not talking about the creation of Adam and Eve. The bible reveals to us a people created into newness of life in II Corinthians 5:17

*'If any man be in Christ he is a new creature, old things have passed away, behold all things have become new.'*

The Lord Jesus paid the price for our salvation. Hence he is able to call us his brethren. He declared the generation by the demonstration of power. He released a secret of heaven that places us above principalities and powers. That we are his seed whom he paid the price of death for is clear in the bible. It is not a surprise to read a prophetic word concerning the Lord and his children and what they are supposed to be in Isaiah 8:18:

*'I and the children whom the Lord had given me are for signs and for wonders.'*

## We are for Signs and Wonders

The issue of his bringing forth is made clear in this verse of scriptures and the fact that we are to be for signs and wonders. This is the ground upon which we must take off to possess our possessions. Outside of this grace, nothing else will work. The provision has already been made for us to manifest as signs and wonders, but the question before us is where are the signs? Where are the wonders? Even though we quote freely Obadiah 18:

*'But upon mount Zion there shall be deliverance, there shall be holiness and the house of Jacob shall possess their possessions'*

What have we possessed? Are we known on Mt Zion? Do we have a place there? What of holiness, is it our watchword? I want you to know that without faith no man can please him and without holiness no man can see him. These are very important for survival. It is important to inform you that by faith Jesus himself declared his generation in Psalm 22:22:

*'I will declare thy name unto my brethren: in the midst of the congregation will I praise thee'*

How did he declare his name to his brethren? Through signs and wonders, because "..*at the call of his name every knee should bow.'* People go to powerful or heavily anointed meetings and return home the same, despite their dwelling under the anointing. This is a disaster!

My prayer is that the power of God will make a difference as you plug into the prophetic promise made by the Lord. It is high time we took the battle to the gate and go ahead to:

## DEALING WITH GENERATION WASTERS

*'......declare his righteousness unto a people that shall be born, that he hath done this'* (Ps 22:31)

It is also recorded in Ps 78:4 that:

*'We will not hide them from their children, showing the generation to come the praises of the Lord and his strength and his wonderful works that he has done'*

Some of us give our children the impression that God does not have power anymore. But there was a woman who raised her child with daily teachings that Jesus answers prayers - He is the healer, deliverer, helper, and provider. This woman several years later was diagnosed to have cancer. The moment they told her she broke down and wept like a baby.

Arrangement was however made for her to travel to England, where she was admitted into a London Hospital. After thorough examination, the doctor informed her there was little they could do to save her life. Whatever they do for her would only keep her alive for just two weeks. The woman could not look at anybody's eyes she lifted up her face up and bitter tears gushed out of her eyes. The information was too much for her to handle. Only two weeks to live!

While she was being wheeled out of the examination room the son ran to her, 'Mummy what did the doctor tell you? Did he say you are going to die?' She did not respond to his question, but fastened her eyes on the ceiling. The boy with faith welling up on the inside said 'Mummy remember you told me Jesus answers prayers. Remember he is the healer. Mummy you will not die'.

This compounded her problem; the fact that her son is privy to the bad news brought more tears flowing from the fountain of her eyes. This she had in abundance and her reservoir of tears seemed not to have failed her as she cried all night. Nothing could placate her. She just went on crying non-stop.

The testimony today is that the woman got miraculously healed while waiting for death in that hospital. The voice of her son kept ringing in her ears 'Mummy you will not die' and she hung on to it. This testimony came because the mother gave the boy the legacy of truth. He invested life and truth in her son and she reaped the fruit of divine healing. So teach your child the way he should go. He may be your savior in future, and this Obadiah 21 confirms very unequivocally: *'.. saviours shall come up on mount Zion…'* (the place of prayer and power )

The story of the mother and child reveals the manifestation of God's power and glory in the healing of the woman through faith of the boy in Jesus. Each victory we have over the devil is a testimony or the:

> *"….showing the generation to come the praises of the Lord and his strength and his wonderful works that he has done."* (Ps 78:4)

# Chapter Nine – **POSSESSING YOUR POSSESSION**

1. Lift up your heads, O ye gates; and the king of glory shall come in with me to possess my possessions.

2. I come against the inner caucus of evil men, working against my progress in Jesus name.

3. I repent of any unknown covenants binding my family to poverty and failure.

4. Let every covenant enforcer, limiting my lineage from going forward be burnt by fire.

5. Let every gate shut against me be opened.

6. I neutralize all unknown agreement between my village with satanic gatekeepers.

7. I resist every legal ground that my ancestors had given satanic powers to rule my lineage.

8. Let my people who sit in darkness see the great light and gravitate towards liberty..

9. O Lord, expose every ploy of Satan to bind us in ignorance in Jesus name.

10 I receive discharge and acquittal from the Lord.

# Chapter Ten
# UPON MOUNT ZION

*'...a river, the streams whereof shall make glad the city of God, the holy place of the tabernacle of the most High' (Ps 46:4).*

## *Introduction*

The city of Zion in the bible is associated basically with deliverance, salvation, Joy, peace etc. It came up uniquely for mentioning when the salvation of Israel became an issue. No matter how bad your case is, as soon as you get into Zion the problem is solved. This is because upon mount Zion there shall be deliverance. So in Ps 53:6 we see a man thinking aloud in expression of a deep-rooted desire. *'Oh that the salvation of Israel were come out of Zion!'*

Why? This is because all hopes were reposed in Zion. There is no help from other sources. Seeking help from somewhere else is nothing but trusting in the arm of the flesh. The mountain of Zion is a place of power, and there mighty men are raised. No wonder the Bible says:

*'And saviours shall come up on mount Zion to judge the mountain of Esau; and the kingdoms shall be the Lord's'* (Oba 21).

It is mandatory that saviors come to the mountain of prayers to bring deliverance to those oppressed by the Esau company. These saviors are intercessors who spend their lives standing in the gap for others. It is important to mention that for every one that goes up to mount Zion there is a mountain of Esau waiting there to resist, but you must make up your mind to judge it.

It seems as one problem is solved another tries to raise its head; this is a revelatory confirmation of the fact that Satan is restless and goes to and fro looking for whom to devour. We see a lamentation in Psalm 3:1

*'Lord, how are they increased that trouble me! Many are they that rise up against me.'*

This is Satan's major pre-occupation. The solution is to turn it over to the Lord, through violent and unrelenting prayers. We see what the man in Psalm 3:4 had to do:

*'I cried unto the Lord with my voice, and he heard me out of his holy hill. (Mount Zion)'*

The deliverance was so rapid and revealing that the man was able to sleep in peace because the Lord sustained him. The assurance of deliverance drove away fear and anxiety and hope and trust were built on God.

No wander the Psalmist in assured confirmation hinted further in Ps 53:6 that

*'...When God bringeth back the captivity of his people, Jacob shall rejoice, and Israel shall be glad'*

He had come to know God as the deliverer and helper and nothing else can suffice. Except a man look unto him, he will forever remain mincemeat in the hand of Satan. It is divine wisdom to set one's heart and mind on him. In Isaiah 45:22 this counsel is clear

*'Look unto me, and be ye saved, all the ends of the earth: for I am God, and there is none else'.*

He is the author and finisher of our faith.

## *Deliverance*

When you closely examine the statement of the Psalmist in chapter 53:6 you will discover it is more of a prayer request than mere statement of fact. This is a clear expression of desperate wish and assertion of the benefit that would come out of this desire.

*'Oh that the salvation of Israel were come out of Zion!'.*

The secret of deliverance is aggressive prayer action and consistent rejection of one's oppressive condition not mere wishing. The situation degenerated into a terrible situation that they were totally broken down by the problems they faced. They accepted their fate, and sat beside the rivers of Babylon and wept as they remembered Zion.

However, they that took them captive required from them a song, but they lamented that how could they sing the Lord's song in a strange land. (Ps 137:1-4) The problem was not the strange land but the fact that

> ***'We hanged our harps upon the willows in the midst thereof*** ('v2).

Now tell me how could they sing if the instrument of worship had been hung upon the willows. Many today are suffering because of actions like this.

Unknown to them, it was this strange land that they needed to sing for their breakthrough to come. Paul and Silas did in a strange land (prison) and the chains and shackles binding them gave way after the Holy Spirit manifested in earthquake. (Acts 16:25-26). There is no strange land with our God wherever and whenever you call he will answer. This is a sad thing, if it takes an unbeliever to ask you where is your God. That Psalm says

> ***'...and they that wasted us required of us mirth, saying Sing us one of the songs of Zion'***

## DEALING WITH GENERATION WASTERS

Notice the word *'wasted'*, the enemies of their souls now tormenting them to sing in the midst of crises. Do not wait for the enemy to ask you to sing. Pick up your harp again and begin to sing. It shall be well with you. There is no strange land with our God, for your breakthrough will come if you sing in the so called strange land. Just like. Paul and Silas were delivered from the power of the prison and their chains and shackles gave way after the Holy Spirit manifested in earthquake, let your singing bring down his presence and cause things to begin to happen for you. There is no strange land with our God wherever and whenever you call he will answer.

## *The River Of Life*

As mentioned earlier, Mount of Zion has been a significant place in the heart of God. God desires it for victory for his people. The city of Zion itself is unique in many respects, that is why you see a lot of references to this great city of God. In it is:

> *'...a river, the streams whereof shall make glad the city of God, the holy place of the tabernacle of the most High'* (Ps 46:4).

The almighty God deliberately put the river in Zion and except you belong to Zion you may never experience the joy or gladness this water can give. The water in Zion does not only refresh and quench thirst it is the kind of water that a man drinks and will never thirst any more.

In addition, the water is not collected just anywhere, the giver or supplier is the Lord Jesus Christ. The encounter with the women at the well in the gospel of John chapter 4 confirms this and also reveals the importance of this water:

> *'...Whosoever drinketh of this water shall thirst again: But whosoever drinketh of the water which I shall give him shall never thirst; but the water that I shall give him shall be in him a well of water springing up into everlasting life'.*
> (John 4:13-14)

What was the reaction of the woman Jesus was talking with? Of course, she wanted the water so that she would not come back again to fetch (John 4:15). Unfortunately for her, the water can neither be given to the unsaved nor be a replacement for domestic use.

It is a known fact that no man can survive without water, because it is a major constituent in the human body formation. So the woman actually did not understand the trend of the discussion, it was spiritual not carnal. The Lord Jesus had the in depth idea of where he was going. The scriptures in Isaiah had revealed the source of water of life and our reaction as we draw from it.

On close examination of the book of Isaiah 12:3 precisely, you will see the reference to this encounter, hence the discussion he had with the women at the well was quite symbolic and expressive of this prophecy.

## DEALING WITH GENERATION WASTERS

***'Therefore with joy shall ye draw water out of the wells of salvation'.***

This woman was willing to pay any price to draw out of this well with joy.

It is necessary to mention that the water can only be drawn '.... ***out of the wells of salvation'***, this is the key that enables the release of its flow into a person's life. This woman must be saved in order for her to draw freely from this well of salvation. The well she stood by was symbolic and the master had made her to see the difference between the water she was about to draw and that which he wanted to give her. The Lord wanted to help her through the way, and path where the water could be drawn, hence, it was in the fulfillment of this that the Lord had to tell her

***'...Go and call thy husband, and come hither to draw.'*** (John 4:16).

From the discussion that followed we could see the honesty of the woman, her confession and acceptance of the account of Jesus concerning her past life. On the spur of the moment the woman not only believed Jesus' testimony about his being the messiah, she left her pot (worldly possession) and went about to proclaim:

***'Come, see a man, which told me all things that ever I did: is not this the Christ?'*** (John 4:29)

The interesting thing here was that within a matter of moment this woman became transformed and received grace to evangelize the city. While Jesus' disciples were busy pursuing the agenda of food, the woman was busy proclaiming Christ to the city. They were more concerned with Jesus eating than proclaiming Christ. While they saw his refusal, they began to wonder whether somebody had come to give him food. The answer of the Lord should have opened their understanding to the subject matter at hand, but because the flesh always resist the spirit they lost the hint.

> *'Jesus saith unto them, My meat is to do the will of him that sent me, and to finish his work'* (John 4:34).

## Laborers Are Few

What was the master saying here in effect? It is simply the fact that his desire is to see souls won into the kingdom of God, than to engage in wining and dining, for this is the will of God. He was determined to finish the work, not concentrate on food. He unraveled the riddle by saying:

> *'...behold I say unto you. Lift up your eyes, and look on the fields; for they are white already to harvest'.* (John 4:35).

Yet they neither saw what he saw through spiritual eyes nor caught the vision expounded to them. What a disaster?

Even though the disciples had long been with Jesus, they had not been able to catch the vision and the ministry of water of life in the way this woman entered into it '.... ***with joy (she drew) water out of the wells of salvation*** ' and the results were unbelievable. However, we may not be far from been correct if we said she actually drank out of that water of life freely, the reason being the result of her testimony:

> *'And many of the Samaritans of that city believed on him for the saying of the woman, which testified...'* (John 4:39).

The utterance that followed her encounter with Jesus confirms the statement of the Lord in Acts 1:8:

> *'But ye shall receive power, after that the Holy Ghost is come upon you: and ye shall be witnesses unto me both in Jerusalem, and in all Judea, and in Samaria, and unto the uttermost part of the earth'.*

It was not an accident that Samaria was mentioned. Why? A woman had been faithful enough to raise several witnesses for Jesus in Samaria and they all believed. Not only that:

> *'And many more believed because of his own word; and said unto the woman, Now we believe, not because of thy saying: for we have heard him ourselves, and know that this is indeed the Christ, the Saviour of the world'.* (John 4:41-42)

## The Refreshing

Now what is this river or water that flows through Zion that makes the people thereof glad? In the gospel of John chapter 7: 37 we see a revelation that the Lord Jesus released to his church.

*'In the last day, that great day of the feast, Jesus stood and cried, saying, if any man thirst, let him come unto me and drink.'*

Here was an open invitation to come and quench ones thirst, it was a call to salvation, and here the word was a vehicle to its fulfillment. The choice is there for any one to make, it is not by force because you must believe. Furthermore, he said:

*'He that believeth on me, as the scripture hath said, out of his belly shall flow rivers of living water'*

The act of believing is the bedrock for the flow of this water. Hence, the Bible declares that

*'The spirit of man is the candle of the Lord, searching the inward parts of the belly'* (Prov 20:27).

Of course, you know the belly under discussion is not a reference to the stomach where food is stored in the body. It is the spirit or heart and in some cases the soul of man. With this understanding, it becomes clear that any believer that drinks of this water out of him shall flow unlimited powers to do the works of God as we

*DEALING WITH GENERATION WASTERS*

saw in the case of the woman of Samaria. (Also refer to John 14:12' greater works than this shall he do.)

The source of this unlimited power is the same reference to water we have been expounding:

*(But spake he of the spirit, which they that believe shall receive: for the Holy Ghost was not yet given: because that Jesus was not yet glorified John* (7:39).)

From this verse of scripture it is clear that it is the Holy Sprit, which all they that believe must receive.

## *Revival or Survival Testimonies?*

What testimonies do you give or what testimonies do you intend to give. The woman at the well introduced a new dimension to giving testimonies. She challenged others with her testimonies and gave matter -of-fact account of what she experienced. Her testimony produced a revival that forced others to seek for the kingdom of God. What a wonderful encounter with a woman who thirsted after righteousness within a short time of her encounter with the master.

These are the days when people come to church to give survival testimonies instead of revival testimonies. When they come, they introduce their testimonies with long praise the Lord! You hear something like this. 'I have been believing God for a house, but now the Lord has done it praise the Lord'. Now there is nothing wrong with this. But most of the time the truth behind the testimony is concealed. One after the other you hear that of provisions of jobs, cars, life partners, money, promotions, etc.

You will not hear frequently testimonies like 'I have been waiting on the Lord for the salvation of my boss for several years. But I wish to testify to the glory of God today, that he is not only saved but baptized in the holy spirit'. You do not hear of people seeking his face for gifts of the spirits but are now operating in them. Neither do you hear testimonies of waiting on God to overcome a dangerous character flaw. No! Revival testimonies are scarce and this speaks volume about the foundation or depth of our faith as Christians today. We are not better than the gentiles. Mt 6:31 tells us

***'Seek ye first the kingdom of God and his righteousness and all these other things shall follow you'.***

Many go at length to seek these things first and falsify testimonies clinically presented in a way to help God achieve false claims.

Many of us are mundane in ideas and focus. Hence, our thoughts are guided by physical gains than spiritual gains. Christians who are kingdom focused desire more from seeing God fulfilling his goals on earth than man fulfilling his desires. They desire that God's will be done and they bend more to this side. A man that seeks the kingdom of God has these blessings pursuing him.

## DEALING WITH GENERATION WASTERS

I knew a brother in Christ, whom I met in one of the house fellowships conducted several years ago. He applied for an international job in a blue chip company and left the handling at the discretion of the company. This was after they had collected his relevant papers and consulted with relevant people abroad. He was not desperate, because he had made adequate consultations with the Lord that answers prayers. He gave the company the information the way it was. They saw his sincerity and against all odds issued him a letter of employment. When they did not hear from him, they sent a courier to pursue him with this 'much sought after gold'.

Yet those who are desperate and do everything to manipulate information do not always make it. God is with the upright and stands with them in the day of trouble. As a child of God, you have grace in the place of prayer to ask and you shall receive. Do not wait for the wasters to ask you to sing. Pick up your hung harp again and begin to sing. There is no strange land with our God, for your breakthrough will come if you sing in the strange land of your destiny.

Let your songs bring down his presence and cause things to begin to happen for you. Allow the Lord bring deliverance from the power of generation wasters as you sing. I believe that the prison, the chains and shackles will give way after the Holy Spirit has manifested in earthquake. There is no strange land with our God wherever and whenever you call he will answer. Order the course of your life on your knees and you will see things begin to happen. God Bless you.

## *Prayer of Commitment/Decision.*

"Oh Lord, I _____ commit myself today, to live a life of prayers, where the things of the kingdom will reign supreme in my heart. Let the spirit of grace and supplication come upon me O Lord and make me a waiter that will achieve kingdom goals on your behalf. Then I shall remain dependable to commit prayer resources to divine economy as you use me. So help me God."

"God Bless you. Now that you have finished praying take a further step by writing your decision on the first blank page of your Bible e.g. **I _____ _____ promise to pray for a minimum of one hour (or more by choice) every day.**"

Sign the date and time that is the month, day, and year. I assure you will never be the same again from today. Amen.

# Chapter Ten – UPON MOUNT ZION

1. I uncover every veil preventing me from identifying my inheritance in Jesus name

2. I forcefully remove every satanic umbrella preventing the rain of blessing to fall on me in Jesus name.

3. I desecrate and render impotent every satanic altar raised against me in Jesus name.

4. In the name of Jesus, I cancel whatever sorrow, tears and bloodshed the enemy had prepared for me.

5. With the shield of faith I intercept all satanic arrows of rejection and hatred shot at me in Jesus name

6. I erase with the blood of Jesus every invisible mark of failure and limitations placed on my lineage.

7. I receive grace for a turn around in blessings, prosperity, favour and health in my life and business in Jesus name.

8. I command every snare set for me to be broken now.

9. I forbid frustration and failure at the point of success.

10. I resist every terror and pestilence satanically projected to any member of my family or me.name.

# Appendix

## *References*

1. **Smashing the Gates of the enemy –** *through strategic prayers.*

2. **TELL Magazine, April 8th 1996**

3. **The Nelson New Illustrated Bible Dictionary.**

4. **Dakes Annotated Reference Bible**

5. **Foxe's Book of Matyrs titled 'History of Christian Matyrs To The General Persecutions Under Nero' by John Foxe.**

## Other books by the Author

i) **Fighting Your Way To Victory (*Principles of Victory over stubborn problems*)**

ii) **Smashing the Gates of the enemy –** *through strategic prayers*

iii) **The Secrets of prevailing in Prayer**

iv) **The gates of hell shall not Prevail Part I**

v) **The gates of hell shall not Prevail Part II**

# Contact

**To Contact Taiwo Ayeni
For speaking engagements
Please write or call**

**e:mail – taayeni@yahoo.com**

**Or**

**Rehoboth Ministries
2822 S State Highway 360 #925
Grand Prairie, Texas, 75052**

**Phones: 972-602- 1837
972-742- 7365**

## About the author

Pastor Taiye Ayeni as he is fondly called, met with the Lord in his final year at the university of Lagos, Akoka, where he graduated with a Bachelors of Science combined honours degree in Mass Communication, Sociology and Psychology.

Since knowing the Lord in 1983, he has been privileged to serve Him in various capacities. He is the Minister in Charge of Rehoboth Ministries, based in Grand Prairie Texas, USA and a Senior Lecturer at the Gethsemane Prayer Ministries International' Prayer School, with its headquarters in Ibadan, Nigeria.

He serves as the Minister in Charge of Prayer at Household Of Faith, of The Redeemed Christian Church of God (RCCG) Arlington, Texas, USA. He is presently in the United States of America on mission for Christ, a student of Advance Leadership and Pastoral School of Christ For The Nations Institute (CFNI) Dallas and mentoree of the prestigious Longridge Writers Group, in Connecticut. He has widely traveled on speaking engagements within and outside the country in the course of ministry work.

He is married to Dr (Mrs.) Abidemi Olubisi Ayeni and the union produced Rereloluwa (son) and Oreoluwa (daughter).

in the United States
VS00001B/1-102

9 781420 817942